This Good Mews is for

_____

May these stories inspire you
to a deeper love of cats
and their Magnificent Creator

In loving memory
of my husband, Jerry

good mews

kitty chappell

inspurrrrational stories for cat lovers

THOMAS NELSON
Since 1798

NASHVILLE   DALLAS   MEXICO CITY   RIO DE JANEIRO   BEIJING

Published in Nashville, TN, by Thomas Nelson.
Thomas Nelson is a trademark of Thomas Nelson, Inc.

Thomas Nelson, Inc., titles may be purchased in bulk for
educational, business, fundraising, or sales promotional use.
For information, please email SpecialMarkets@ThomasNelson.com.

Designed by Thinkpen Design, LLC

ISBN-10: 1-4041-8709-x
ISBN-13: 978-1-4041-8709-2

Printed in China

ACKNOWLEDGMENTS

WITH DEEP GRATITUDE TO:

The coworker at Southern California Gas Company in Santa Barbara, California, who provided us with our first cat, Curiosity

Hank and Arlene Norcutt, who brightened our lives with Smokey

Millie Riebe, who, amidst her busy bookkeeping duties, took care of Single Strength and his siblings after they were found abandoned by their mother cat in the office loft

Rose Gorrel, who through tears entrusted her beloved El Gato Gordo to us when she moved to a place that didn't allow pets

Steve and Genie Burnell, who gave up their cherished Miss Middy so she could find the perfect place

Our daughter, Tamara, our son, David, and our granddaughter, Bailey, who've loved our cats dearly

My sister, Chris, who shared stories of her Skeeter and Taz

SPECIAL GRATITUDE TO:

Mark Gilroy and Thomas Nelson Publishers for making this book a reality

Kathy Baker, editor, who has four cats of her own—qualifying her to be the purr-fect editor for this book. Great job, Kathy!

MEGA THANKS TO:

All of you cat-loving friends who take time to read this book!

I welcome your comments: www.kittychappell.com

Table of Contents

Foreword

Cat lovers are special people. We can be snubbed and not take it personally (which, when you think about it, puts us in a good position to make it through life). We can pretend we don't smell kitty litter when it's five feet away (even though it's wilting the house plants). We don't mind a furry creature coming along and plopping itself down on the paper we happen to be reading, or jumping at us from some unexpected location (and giving us a near coronary) just because he or she wants to play. We'll give up our favorite chair simply because our cat got first dibs. And we are fluent in "purr" and can carry on conversations with our pet that no one else understands. Yes, cat lovers are special people.

That is why this is the perfect book for cat lovers. It not only talks about the world we've all come to know and love, the world of cats, but it reminds us of how much our cats teach us.

Here is just a few of the things that I've learned from the cats who have been part of our family over the years:

- *No goal is too high.* When I think of the places to which our cats have climbed, I am amazed. Construction workers even with their ladders wouldn't be so daring. If a cat wants to venture someplace, he or she will find some way to get there.

- *Ask for what you want.* Cats don't just sit there and wait for life to bring them the things that they want. They boldly ask for them. They will get right in your face and keep purring until you get up and meet their needs.

- *You don't always need others' approval.* Cats are comfortable in their own fur. When it comes to certain people, they can take them or leave them. They don't sit in the corner wondering if someone likes or approves of them. They just go on with their lives, confident of their worth, regardless of someone else's bias or judgment.

- *Cats make their presence known.* In one way or another, you know a cat is in a house, either from their quiet purring, a sudden pounce, or the fact that they're sitting in your favorite chair.

- *Cats never forget how to play.* No matter how old they are, a string, a ball, or a squeaky toy can usually get them up on their feet and into play mode. How many of us can say the same thing? For many of us, the last exercise we got was signing the membership forms to a health club that we haven't used since.

I've learned a lot of other things from my cats over the years. But I'd much rather let Kitty Chappell and her fun new book *Good Mews* tell you more about cats, about cat lovers, and about the God who created us all.

Martha Bolton

*Author of more than 50 books and comedy writer
for performers such as Bob Hope, Phyllis Diller,
Ann Jillian, Jeff Allen, and Mark Lowry*

Preface

Move Over, Rover!

AS INTELLIGENT AS EACH OF OUR CATS WERE, NONE OF THEM COULD
WRITE. HAD THEY THAT ABILITY, HOWEVER, I AM CERTAIN THEY WOULD
HAVE PUT THEIR HEADS TOGETHER AND WRITTEN SOMETHING SIMILAR TO
WHAT IS WRITTEN BELOW AS A PREFACE FOR THIS BOOK.

Move over, Rover! It's true that every dog has his day, but yours are
over. Latest statistics show what we cats, with our superior intellect, have
anticipated all along. Man has a new best friend—cats. You are no longer
top dog!

Sure, you slobbered and drooled all over your owners, you fetched
their smelly slippers, you dashed into the heat and cold and dragged in
heavy newspapers. You played their silly games. You rolled over and
played dead and begged for fake bones. Purr-lease! Have you no dignity?
And then you pulled your tail under your belly like a coward and groveled
even after some of your owners mistreated you. Have you no self-respect?

And what were we cats doing all this time? We were sitting in the
window, aloof from the world, contemplating weightier matters of the
universe, waiting for our day to come. Well, it's here!

You said cats were dumb because we refused to play your silly games.
Don't you know that we have a few tricks of our own? Some of us can
fetch (those of us who are more into athletics). Some of us can jump up
and turn on light switches. Some of us can open the door by turning the
knob. Some of us have actually been potty trained to go on the toilet.

(Show us one dog in God's whole earth who can do that!) And some of us can even write a foreword to a book. And we don't even need spell check!

Face it, we are the better house pet. You dogs run around relieving yourself wherever you feel like it and don't even have the class to cover it up. Or you drink out of places you have no business putting your mouth. And you're so codependent you have to train your hard-working, loyal masters to carry little scoopers around and clean up behind you. What kind of a friend is that?

I know, I know. We have our faults too. We carefully cover our droppings in flowerbeds and gardens where unsuspecting hands discover them when working in the soil. (Well, we can't be purrfect!) And, yes, we also play seemingly silly games.

We chase strings that are pulled by our people, and we jump up and try to grab things they dangle above us. But only if we're in the mood. Besides, we have a reason for participating in these activities. They help us to develop stronger muscles and better motor skills, which aid us in ridding our people's homes of wild critters such as moths, lizards, and pesky mice. (And okay, we confess, sometimes our motives are to rid the house of you dogs too!)

But with good reason. We're not the ones keeping our neighbors awake with incessant barking. We may yowl from time to time to attract a lover, or to tell off another feline (who may be trying to move in on our date), but that's the extent of our disruption of the stillness. We certainly have never been accused of howling at the moon! (By the way, why do you do that? Look, the moon comes out practically every night. Get over it!)

Yet we must admit that with all of our differences, a couple of cats (Curiosity and Smokey, whom you are about to meet) had a best friend named Ali, a dog. They grew up together, played together, and even slept together. They felt quite protected when Ali was around. They really missed him when he moved away. You see, we have been known to cut you dogs some slack now and then, and in some cases we even kind of love you.

So don't be too sad that we are now first place in the lives of humans. Who knows how long we will stay there? The simple truth is this—God placed dogs and cats alike on earth with a special mission: We are to provide unconditional God-like love and support to our people, help them understand us more, and, in the process, maybe help them understand themselves a little better too.

IN ORDER TO KEEP A TRUE PERSPECTIVE
OF ONE'S IMPORTANCE, EVERYONE SHOULD
HAVE A DOG THAT WILL WORSHIP HIM AND
A CAT THAT WILL IGNORE HIM.

DEREKE RITA

DOGS BELIEVE THEY ARE HUMAN.
CATS BELIEVE THEY ARE GOD.

JEFF VALDEZ

YOU CAN KEEP A DOG;
BUT IT IS THE CAT WHO KEEPS PEOPLE,
BECAUSE CATS FIND HUMANS
USEFUL DOMESTIC ANIMALS.

GEORGE MIKES

What a Mess!

I arrived home from work one evening to a living room scattered with debris. I followed a trail of white ribbons, semi-folded gift boxes, and rumpled tissues that led into our bedroom. I knew Curiosity, our beloved cat, was the creator of this mess, but where was he?

I peered under our bed, an old frame handcrafted by my father, which sat high off the floor. In the space beneath it were nested boxes and ribbons that had contained our wedding gifts three months earlier. An oversized bedspread reached to the floor and hid this storage area—the perfect spot for an inquisitive kitten. But Ross (Curiosity's nickname) wasn't there.

I called, but there was still no answer. As my eyes scanned the room, I noted a slight movement of the sheer window curtains. On the other side of the bed, at the foot of the curtains, I discovered a tiny gift box stuffed with Ross, squashed tightly, backside down, with all four feet up in the air. For entertainment, he was swatting his tail as it dangled above his nose.

"What a mess!" I exclaimed, pulling him from the box. "How on earth did you ever get yourself into such a fix?"

Without a meow of response, he bounded for his water bowl and litter box. However long he had been stuck in his cramped quarters or however he got there, he sure was excited to finally be free!

Like Ross, I was once in a very tight spot. I found myself stuffed in a sinful condition that I could not get out of without help. Only Someone with strong, gentle hands, the desire to find me, and a heart full of love could lift me out of my hopeless situation. I would have been stuck there for a long time—for all eternity—if Christ hadn't rescued me.

Thank You, Lord, for loving me enough to reach down and lift me out of my helpless condition. And thank You for helping me the second time, the third time, the fourth . . . Amen

He brought me out into a spacious place;
he rescued me because he delighted in me.

PSALM 18:19 NIV

A KITTEN IS CHIEFLY REMARKABLE
FOR RUSHING ABOUT LIKE MAD
AT NOTHING WHATEVER,
AND GENERALLY STOPPING
BEFORE IT GETS THERE.

AGNES REPPLIER

WHEN YOU INVITE A KITTEN
INTO YOUR HOME, YOU BRING
INDOORS SOMETHING SLIGHTLY WILD,
OFTEN UNPREDICTABLE,
AND ALWAYS ENTERTAINING.

BARBARA L. DIAMOND

A CAT WILL ASSUME THE
SHAPE OF ITS CONTAINER.

ANONYMOUS

Trophies

Curiosity grew to be a twenty-two-pound, strawberry-blond, long-haired feline who loved to bring me surprise gifts. These included early morning love offerings of beheaded gophers and half-eaten rats, carefully placed on the front doormat just where my foot would land. How could he know that instead of bringing me joy, his trophies filled me only with disgust?

I'm sure he worked hard, waiting, creeping, pouncing, and stalking through the night. But couldn't he find better ways to show his love for me? For example, happily eating whatever was placed before him, using his scratching post instead of my furniture, and not fighting with his next-door friend at two in the morning! Even cozying up next to me as I sat and watched television would be better than these rodent-of-the-month club deliveries.

That made me wonder: What do I offer the Lord to show my love for Him? Do I give Him something less than my best efforts? I boast of my gift of almost perfect church attendance, but how faithful am I in attending to the more perfect gifts He prefers to receive, such as loving my neighbor and forgiving those who wrong me?

Anyone can attend church. Attending to His commandment of forgiving old wounds, especially ones you didn't deserve, is another matter entirely. And sure, I've read the Bible from cover to cover, not missing a word. But how much of His Word can He read in me?

Maybe I'll think more about this the next time I look down with disdain on another love offering from my cat.

Lord, forgive me for offering You partial sacrifices—the parts that feed my childish ego but which You can't fully use. Help me to cultivate the offering that would be the perfect gift for You: a pure motive.

The Lord says,
"I do not want all these sacrifices.
I have had enough. . . . Don't continue
bringing me worthless sacrifices!"

ISAIAH 1:11, 13 NCV

EVEN OVERWEIGHT
CATS INSTINCTIVELY KNOW
THE CARDINAL RULE:
WHEN FAT, ARRANGE
YOURSELF IN SLIM POSES.

JOHN WEITZ

I'VE MET MANY THINKERS
AND MANY CATS,
BUT THE WISDOM OF CATS
IS INFINITELY SUPERIOR.

HIPPOLYTE TAINE

A CAT IS A TIGER
THAT IS FED BY HAND.

VAKAOKA GENRIN

Is Seeing Believing?

As I left my front yard, Ross fell into step beside me. "You stay here," I said. "You don't need to walk me to my friend's house. It's blocks away. Besides, you can't go in. You will have to stay outside until I come back out." But Ross insisted.

I didn't mind his padding along beside me. I enjoyed his company. What I did mind was how he sat on the front step and yowled loudly the entire length of my stay, disrupting the stillness of the neighborhood. Because he could not see me, I guess he thought I had abandoned him. Silly cat!

There are times when I, too, walk in unfamiliar places. Because I cannot "see" my heavenly Father, I become afraid. "Where are You, Lord?" I yowl mournfully, disrupting the peace of those around me. I sometimes forget His promise about never forsaking me.

Silly me!

Lord, forgive me when I doubt Your
presence in unfamiliar circumstances.
Remind me that regardless of where
I am, You are always there with me.
I can live in peace and quit my nervous
yowling. Amen

[God] Himself has said,
"I will never leave you nor forsake you."
HEBREWS 13:5 NKJV

WHEN YOU'RE SPECIAL TO A CAT,
YOU'RE SPECIAL INDEED. . . .
SHE BRINGS TO YOU THE GIFT OF
HER PREFERENCE OF YOU,
THE SIGHT OF YOU,
THE SOUND OF YOUR VOICE,
THE TOUCH OF YOUR HAND.

LEONORE FLEISHER

CATS ARE ENDLESS OPPORTUNITIES
FOR REVELATION.

LESLIE KAPP

WHO AMONG US HASN'T ENVIED
A CAT'S ABILITY TO IGNORE THE CARES
OF DAILY LIFE AND TO RELAX COMPLETELY?

KAREN BRADEMEYER

Out on a Limb

"Oh, don't worry about your kitten getting up in a tree and not being able to come back down. That's what cats do best," my friend said with authority. "I don't know why people make such a fuss about kittens in trees. I guarantee you they'll come down when they get hungry enough."

It made sense to me, especially after I heard it a number of times from other individuals. Our Smokey, a fluffy gray puff of smoke, was only a few months old, and I worried about him. We lived high upon a hill with tall trees that lined the long driveway, where huge owls often sat at night and called to each other. It was just a simple house with a simple family—but he was a very special little kitten to us all.

One late afternoon, he did not respond to my usual call. I called out his name loudly and repeatedly, the fear now welling up in my chest. Still no answer. I alerted everyone and as a family we called and searched, but Smokey was nowhere to be found.

The next morning we retraced our steps, calling and searching, but still no Smokey. Heavyhearted, we went our separate ways into the day's activities.

The first day and night were long; the second day and night were an eternity. We grieved silently, fearing the worst.

The next morning, my husband, Jerry, again walked down our long driveway, calling Smokey's name. Suddenly, he heard a faint, weak cry. He followed the sounds to the foot of a tall eucalyptus tree where he looked up and saw a frightened, cold, shivering Smokey clinging to one of the limbs.

He brought the tallest ladder he could find and, with great difficulty, rescued the fear-paralyzed kitten.

Once safe inside our home, Smokey relaxed. After drinking his fill of warm milk, he drifted into a peaceful sleep in the arms of the one who had saved him.

Our son, David, and our daughter, Tamara, discussed with Jerry and me the false sense of security we had first experienced because we believed the words of those who didn't really know what they were talking about on the subject of kittens and trees. So much for the wisdom of man, we concluded.

It reminded me of those people who say it doesn't matter which spiritual tree we climb, since any tree will get us to heaven. They say there's no need for a Savior and if we're smart, we'll select the tree that is the easiest to climb.

But these individuals don't know what they are talking about. The fact is we do need a Savior. Each of us is lost and helpless out on the limb of life until our heavenly Father rescues us—not because of the tree we are in, but because of the One who allowed Himself to be nailed to a tree two thousand years ago. No cry is too weak for Him to hear, and when He rescues us, we, too, can rest safely in His arms for all eternity. Maybe then we'll think twice before venturing up the wrong tree again.

Thank You, Father, that the only tree needed to access Your Kingdom is the Tree of Life. Help me to not trust the wisdom of man but to lean completely upon the Truth as revealed in Your Word. Amen

Jesus answered, "I am the way, the truth, and the life. No one comes to the Father except through me."

JOHN 14:6 NKJV

A CAT CAN CLIMB DOWN FROM A TREE
WITHOUT THE ASSISTANCE OF THE
FIRE DEPARTMENT OR ANY OTHER AGENCY.
THE PROOF IS THAT NO ONE HAS EVER
SEEN A CAT SKELETON IN A TREE.

ANONYMOUS

IF YOUR CAT FALLS OUT OF A TREE,
GO INDOORS TO LAUGH.

PATRICIA HITCHCOCK

KITTENS CAN HAPPEN TO ANYONE.

PAUL GALLICO

Whose Job?

Smokey was not a mouser. If a mouse ran across his path, and if it were close enough, he'd reach out and swat at it. If he caught it, he would bat it around and play with it, but he would never eat it. He had more gourmet tastes. Besides, you never knew where that mouse had been. So, I set out mouse traps.

One morning, Smokey entered the kitchen as I emptied a trap, and he indicated he wanted the mouse. I led him to the door and tossed the mouse outside. It was dead, but Smokey pretended it wasn't. He tossed it into the air, pounced on it, ignored it, and then ran behind a bush to stalk it again. He repeated the process the rest of the morning.

Tamara, a teenager at the time, had lots of things in her room for field mice to hide under. The quietness of the evening was sometimes shattered with screams of "Mom, help! There's a mouse in my room. Come get him, quick!"

"What am I, the family mouser?" I would grumble, making my way upstairs. She knew that I had learned as a teenager on my grandmother's farm to catch mice just behind the neck so as not to be bitten.

Smokey, who usually dozed in the corner of Tamara's room, always ignored the mouse—that is, until I arrived. When I stalked the mouse, he became interested. Not enough, however, to move—until I caught the mouse. Then it was the usual "I want the mouse" dance routine as I led him to the front door. Only this time, it was a live mouse.

Although those occasions were rare when he received a mouse from me, dead or alive, one would think it was a daily event. For weeks afterward, each time he came near me he meowed loudly and checked my hands, searching for a mouse. Displaying empty hands never convinced him that I had nothing to

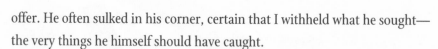

offer. He often sulked in his corner, certain that I withheld what he sought—the very things he himself should have caught.

His behavior reminds me of my own, when I follow the Lord around doing my "I want something" routine. Recently, I've been badgering Him for less stressful circumstances at work and more consideration from certain people.

Maybe what He wants from me is more initiative: toss out irritations, pounce less on mistakes, ignore slights, stalk understanding, and practice patience, instead of just following Him around looking for handouts.

Sure, He will help me. But there are some things He expects me to do for myself!

Lord, remind me that the irritating people and circumstances I try to avoid provide "opportunities in work clothes." Encourage me as I leave my cozy corner and start doing the things You expect of me. Amen

My brothers and sisters, when you have many kinds of troubles, you should be full of joy, because you know that these troubles test your faith, and this will give you patience. Let your patience show itself perfectly in what you do. Then you will be perfect and complete and will have everything you need.

JAMES 1:2-4 NCV

THE SMALLEST FELINE IS A MASTERPIECE.

LEONARDO DA VINCI

ANY CAT WHO MISSES A MOUSE PRETENDS
IT WAS AIMING FOR THE DEAD LEAF.

CHARLOTTE GRAY

ONE REASON WE ADMIRE CATS IS FOR
THEIR PROFICIENCY IN ONE-UPMANSHIP.
THEY ALWAYS SEEM TO COME OUT ON TOP,
NO MATTER WHAT THEY ARE DOING,
OR PRETEND THEY DO.

BARBARA WEBSTER

What's in a Name?

"What kind of a name is 'Single Strength Chappell!'" I shouted. "Please, don't name him that," I begged Jerry. "I am the one who will have the chore of explaining his name every day of his nine lives!"

My husband had dragged this pitiful, sickly, runt-of-the-litter kitten home from his office loft where a stray alley cat had snuck in and presented him with a litter of three kittens. But did he also have to give him such a dumb name?

Besides, I was openly miffed that he had not selected the kitten I wanted from the litter—the sleek and healthy brindle. A gorgeous cat! And with so much to offer! (Jerry had named her "Crystal," somewhat better than "Single Strength!")

Each kitten, not yet big enough to fight for its rights, had been named after one of the three types of standard glass used in our commercial glass company at that time: Plate, Crystal, and Single Strength. Luckily for our children, he hadn't used the same naming process on them.

Realizing my ignorance as to the significance of those names, Jerry patiently explained, "Plate glass is the strongest of our three types of glass, crystal is the second strongest, and single strength is the most delicate. Since this kitten was so sickly, we weren't sure he would even make it—that means he was the most delicate. So I named him 'Single Strength.'"

Jerry was adamant about his choice, but I refused to pronounce that name clearly. When calling Single in from outside I slurred the word to make it sound more like "Cinco" to anyone listening. Admittedly, as only mothers would understand, there were times when I took full advantage of his long name: "Single Strength Chappell! Get out of that street!"

I soon fell madly in love with Single and didn't care what his name was. Much to Jerry's disappointment, he could see, as clear as glass, that Single was my cat, for we became inseparable.

I've sometimes wondered whether the angels would have preferred that the King, my heavenly Father, adopt someone else instead of me. Did they see me as puny and sickly with a terminal disease, a runt with a questionable background and nothing to offer? No! The Bible says the angels rejoice over each one of us who comes to know Him. They know that God loves us and accepts us as we are. They've been watching Him do it for thousands of years. I may have been "single strength" when I first accepted Christ into my life, but I've got a new name now. And I'm no longer a weakling—with His help, I'm even stronger than plate glass.

Throughout history, the name of *Christian* has been both mocked and cherished, depending on which side of the cross someone happens to stand. But I love my new name. I'm a Christian! I pray that it fits me well and that I will never bring it shame or underestimate the strength it represents.

Father, help me to live in a manner that is worthy of the name You gave me. May the transparency of the definition of that name be seen so clearly in my life that others will want to join Your family. Amen

Then you will have a new name,
which the LORD himself will give you.

ISAIAH 62:2 NCV

THEY SAY THE TEST OF LITERARY
POWER IS WHETHER A MAN
CAN WRITE AN INSCRIPTION.
I SAY, "CAN HE NAME A KITTEN?"

SAMUEL BUTLER

CATS MUST HAVE THREE NAMES—
AN EVERYDAY NAME, SUCH AS PETER;
A MORE PARTICULAR, DIGNIFIED NAME,
SUCH AS QUAXO, BOMBALURINA, OR JELLYLORUM;
AND, THIRDLY, THE NAME THE CAT THINKS
UP FOR HIMSELF, HIS DEEP AND INSCRUTABLE
SINGULAR NAME.

T. S. ELIOT

A CAT'S NAME MAY TELL YOU
MORE ABOUT ITS OWNERS THAN
IT DOES ABOUT THE CAT.

LINDA W. LEWIS

Hidden Agenda?

Smokey was king of the household until we brought home Single—our eight-week-old bundle of enthusiasm. It is understandable that an older cat would be upset by the arrival of a young upstart, but Single would have been better tolerated had he been born with good manners. Single's free spirit increased with each passing day. No class at all. And no desire to learn the house rules, much less live by them. It was like he thought our home was his frat house and he was there to party!

Smokey had been a gift from my friend Arlene, a devout cat lover who had painstakingly placed each treasure from her mamma cat's litter. Although he'd had his rebellious moments as a youngster, Smokey had quickly developed a respect for rules: No jumping on the sofa, no sitting in the chairs unless invited onto one's lap for loving and stroking, no jumping onto the kitchen counter (no matter how hungry), and definitely no jumping onto the dining room table—which was exactly what Single did this particular afternoon.

Just as I entered the room, Single leaped into the middle of the table, barely missing the centerpiece. Smokey, dozing on the floor a few feet away, opened his eyes and raised his head. He glared at Single, then looked in my direction as if to ask, "Well, what are you going to do about that?"

"That is NO!" I said sharply to Single.

Since the beginning of time in the kingdom of our household, *no* is a word to be respected by cats. It commands instant attention and obedience, otherwise the offending subject is banished to the outside world for a time of serious reflection. And if that's at dinnertime, too bad.

Single had heard the word *no* before, but as he often did, he suddenly developed a case of deafness. I repeated the word again, louder and with more authority. Single began to bathe himself, fully ignoring the movement of my lips. It was obvious all he was hearing was "blah, blah, blah." I was barking out the commands and he was saying, "Talk to the paw!" Smokey now sat at full attention, awaiting the sentencing. He knew Single had broken the rules and that there would be some serious consequences to his behavior.

I picked up a newspaper, rolled it, and swatted the table loudly near Single, who simply moved over a few inches and resumed primping. By that time Smokey was almost in cardiac arrest. He was ready to start calling in the vigilantes if I didn't take care of the matter myself. "Where's the justice?! Where's the justice?!" I could almost hear him growl through his meows.

"Single, NO!" I said sharply as I swatted him lightly on the behind with the paper. Finally getting a clue, Single, in slow motion, sauntered across the table and jumped down.

Smokey looked at Single, and then at me as if to ask, "That's it? That is all you're going to do?" The punishment phase of the trial definitely had not gone as he had expected.

As Single strolled past him, Smokey gave me one last inquiring look. Apparently not satisfied with my passiveness, he suddenly whacked Single on the side of the head with his big paw, bowling him over. Though Single was unscathed, Smokey walked from the room with head and tail high, satisfied at having taken the law into his own paw.

I can relate to Smokey's feelings. I often question God about His lack of action regarding certain people in the King's household who don't always live by His house rules. I feel they should be put in their place with a stronger hand of discipline. Why does He let them get away with so much? There are times when I want to verbally whack them upside the head too. But just when I am tempted to reach out and swat them with my self-righteous judgment, I am reminded of all those times I've arrogantly ignored my Master and arrogantly continued in my bad behavior. I'm also reminded of something Jesus said about casting the first stone. Oops! Maybe it's better to just keep our paws and our self-righteous attitudes to ourselves.

Father, thank You for not giving me what I deserve. If You did, You would either be swatting me all the time, or I would be banished to the outside for all eternity. Please help me to be as patient with others as You are with me. Amen

Why do you judge your brothers or sisters
in Christ? And why do you think you are better
than they are? We will all stand before God to be
judged, because it is written in the Scriptures:
"'As surely as I live,' says the Lord, 'Everyone will
bow before me; everyone will say that I am God.'"
So each of us will have to answer to God. For that
reason we should stop judging each other.

ROMANS 14:10-13 NCV

No animal should ever
jump on the dining room
furniture unless absolutely
certain that he can hold his
own in the conversation.

Fran Lebowitz

Cats' hearing apparatus is built
to allow the human voice to easily
go in one ear and out the other.

Stephen Baker

After scolding one's cat,
one looks into its face and
is seized by the ugly suspicion
that it understood every word.
And has filed it for reference.

Charlotte Gray

A dog, I have always said,
is prose; a cat is a poem.

Jean Burden

Embarrassed!

Single had a fetish for lingerie. Sometimes, when I left in a hurry, my underwear drawer remained slightly open. Without fail this was discovered by Single, who patiently fished out, one by one, anything he could reach. I often returned home to find bras, panties, nightgowns, and slips strewn up and down the curved stairwell—the focal point when the front door was entered. It was most embarrassing when I brought company home with me.

Victoria would have no secret as long as Single was around!

One night, following a movie out with close friends, we invited them home for dessert. Upon opening the front door, all eyes focused upon sundry undies littering the stairs. Nudging Jerry, the other gentleman grinned and asked teasingly, "What's the matter, can't you afford to buy your wife a dryer?"

Masking my embarrassment, I called out, "Single, you brat!"

Single, of course, had no idea how his actions had embarrassed me. He might have even thought he was doing me a favor, helping me sort through my undergarments.

I wonder about my habits—those I know about, and those I am unaware of. Do I, too, leave a tell-tale trail of unmentionables for others to see when they drop in unexpectedly into my life circumstances? Do these bad habits embarrass my heavenly Father? I wonder if He has a different scene in mind that He wants others to see when He brings them into my life without notice.

Lord, help me to so live that I may be faithful to You, regardless of the time or circumstance. May I never be a source of embarrassment to Your holy name. Amen

Be ready in season and out of season.

2 TIMOTHY 4:2 NKJV

CAT LOVERS CAN READILY BE IDENTIFIED.
THEIR CLOTHES ALWAYS LOOK OLD AND
WELL USED. THEIR SHEETS LOOK LIKE
BATH TOWELS, AND THEIR BATH TOWELS LOOK
LIKE A COLLECTION OF KNITTING MISTAKES.

ERIC GURNEY

THE WHOLE WORLD IS A PLAYGROUND,
AND THE CAT IS THE RIGHTFUL ROYALTY THEREIN.

KAREN DUPREY

IF IT'S NOT TIED DOWN, IT'S A CAT TOY.

ANONYMOUS

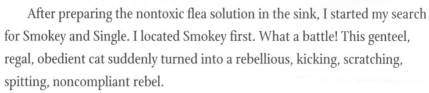

A Love Bath

"It's bath time, guys. Gotta get rid of those fleas!"
I called out to a suddenly empty room.

After preparing the nontoxic flea solution in the sink, I started my search
for Smokey and Single. I located Smokey first. What a battle! This genteel,
regal, obedient cat suddenly turned into a rebellious, kicking, scratching,
spitting, noncompliant rebel.

"Smokey, settle down," I said firmly. "You can either cooperate and we'll
get this job done quickly, or you can struggle and make it twice as long and
hard for both of us. The choice is yours—but you will take this bath." He chose
the second option. After a long battle, the job was finally completed. Once he
was towel-dried, Smokey retreated to a kitchen corner to lick his fur and glare
at me.

I finally located Single, who allowed me to scoop him up and carry him to
the sink. This usually rebellious, high-spirited, mind-of-his-own feline creature
struggled only mildly for a few moments. Then with sad eyes fixed intently
upon my face, he laid his head on the side of my arm and yielded.

Suddenly, I was hit by the truth of the moment. My eyes filled with tears
as I said, "Single, I wish I could be more like you right now, and less like
Smokey." Single, even with his fun-loving and sometimes mischievous nature,
knew how to surrender to his master. How I struggle and fight when I am in
an uncomfortable situation! Single continued to relax on my arm as his eyes
searched my face for understanding.

I recalled my bitter struggle when God had denied me the perfect job in a
place where all the employees were Christians. He placed me, instead, in a firm

where I was the only Christian. How I strove to get out of that situation—an office steeped in immorality, including drug and alcohol abuse.

After only one week, I gave my notice, agreeing to stay until I found another job. Although I received high ratings on tests and interviews for new jobs, it was as though some force held me back. I cried out to God, who told me to be still. Those two little words, *be still*, sure are tough to follow. I went on more job interviews, but nothing happened. With sharp complaints, I lashed out each night at God. I searched the Bible for a reason for His firmness, and I began to notice a pattern: "Love your neighbor as yourself" (Matthew 19:19); "Dear friends, since God so loved us, we also ought to love one another" (1 John 4:11); and finally, "It is not the healthy who need a doctor, but the sick. I have not come to call the righteous, but sinners" (Mark 2:17).

I complained to God that although my coworkers liked me and were kind to me, I was still uncomfortable because I had nothing in common with them. His Word revealed how wrong I was: "While we were still sinners, Christ died for us" (Romans 5:8), and "There is not a righteous man on earth who does what is right and never sins" (Ecclesiastes 7:20). I finally yielded and let God fill me with compassion for an office in which, ultimately, He was exalted.

After towel-drying Single, who immediately ran to play with his favorite toy, I glanced at Smokey, who still sulked in the corner. "That's okay, Smokey, I understand how you feel."

Baths are good for us. Whether it's a bath to clean our bodies or God's love bath to clean up our lives and attitudes, we're always better off to just accept the cleansing, instead of fighting it. And when it's over, we can rejoice like Single because we know we're better for it.

Lord, help me in difficult times to lay my head against Your arm and trust You completely. Amen

Be still, and know that I am God;
I will be exalted.

PSALM 46:10 NKJV

CATS ARE THE ULTIMATE NARCISSISTS.
YOU CAN TELL THIS BY ALL THE TIME
THEY SPEND ON PERSONAL GROOMING.
DOGS AREN'T LIKE THIS. A DOG'S IDEA
OF PERSONAL GROOMING IS TO
ROLL IN A DEAD FISH.

JAMES GORMAN

I GAVE MY CAT A BATH THE
OTHER DAY . . . THEY LOVE IT.
HE SAT THERE, HE ENJOYED IT,
IT WAS FUN FOR ME. THE FUR
WOULD STICK TO MY TONGUE,
BUT OTHER THAN THAT . . .

STEVE MARTIN

TO BATHE A CAT TAKES BRUTE FORCE,
PERSEVERANCE, COURAGE OF CONVICTION—
AND A CAT. THE LAST INGREDIENT IS
USUALLY HARDEST TO COME BY.

STEPHEN BAKER

Go Fetch!

"Anybody got time to play fetch with Single?" I called out loudly.

"Not me," called Tamara from upstairs. "I'm late for school."

"Not me," called David, rushing to the door. "I'm late for work."

"Guess who that leaves?" I grumbled. Single sat patiently in the middle of the kitchen floor, his wadded paper ball prominently displayed in front of him.

Single had learned to fetch quite by accident. To distract him from playing with the extension cord connected to the hair dryer I was using one morning, I had taken a piece of paper tucked inside the book I was reading, wadded it up, and thrown it to the far side of the large bonus room. That should keep him busy for awhile, I reasoned.

Within seconds he had returned and dropped the paper ball in front of me. More interested in the book I was reading than entertaining thoughts of Single learning a new game, I again tossed the ball. It was returned. This time I took notice.

"Cats don't fetch!" I exclaimed. They'll take note of where the ball lands, wonder why in the world you would do such a thing as throw a wadded-up piece of paper across the room, but they won't bother to get up to go get it. But this cat did. In fact, thirteen times Single returned the ball to me. Thus was born a game that brought countless hours of joy for Single, the entire household, and any participating visitors.

But sometimes Single wanted to play fetch when his timing did not fit into my plans. Such was the case this morning. I didn't have time for his usual fifteen-minute-minimum fast-paced game. I could spare only a few minutes. Grabbing his paper ball, I ran up the stairs with Single outrunning me in anticipation. Once at the top, I threw the ball down the stairs. It barely reached the floor when Single's black and white streak retrieved it and bounded back up the stairs, ready for another romp. Playing fetch with him in this manner accomplished two things: It fulfilled my desire to meet his need for an instant game, and did it quickly.

After laboriously climbing the stairs with his final retrieval, Single dropped the ball on the carpet and collapsed beside it. With sides heaving, and panting mouth open, he gave me a look that did not reflect gratitude but clearly said, "Enough!" He was exhausted.

I felt a twinge of guilt. What if God handled our needs in the same way that I had handled Single's—to just rush us through a quick game of fetch to satisfy us? "There's your dream, go get it! Wait, it's not there! It's over here. Now it's over there! Here! There! Go get it!" What if He kept us running around in circles until we wasted all our energy and were so exhausted we didn't care about our dreams anymore? Thankfully, that's not in His character to act that way. He has a distinct plan for our lives and He will reveal it to us in time. We may have to work to fetch it, but He will never have us run after it in vain.

Thank You, Father, for responding
to my needs and not reacting to my
expediency. Thank You for sticking to
Your plan in spite of my doubts and
protests. Your timing is always perfect.
Amen

He has made everything beautiful in its time.

ECCLESIASTES 3:11 NKJV

WHEN I PLAY WITH MY CAT,
WHO KNOWS IF I AM NOT A PASTIME
TO HER MORE THAN SHE IS TO ME?

MICHEL E. DE MONAIGNE

ALTHOUGH ALL CAT GAMES HAVE THEIR RULES
AND RITUALS, THESE VARY WITH THE INDIVIDUAL PLAYER.
THE CAT, OF COURSE, NEVER BREAKS A RULE. IF IT DOES
NOT FOLLOW PRECEDENT, THAT SIMPLY MEANS IT HAS
CREATED A NEW RULE AND IT IS UP TO YOU TO LEARN
IT QUICKLY IF YOU WANT THE GAME TO CONTINUE.

SIDNEY DENHAM

THERE ARE NO ORDINARY CATS.

COLETTE

NO MATTER HOW TIRED OR WRETCHED I AM,
A PUSSYCAT SITTING IN A DOORWAY CAN DIVERT MY MIND.

MARY E. WILKINS FREEMAN

Copy Cat! Copy Cat!

I stopped and listened. There it was again—a strange, muffled moan. I followed the intermittent sounds to the garage and opened the door slowly. Smokey sat before me with head bowed low. He had entered from the side door, which was always left open for him and Single.

"Smokey! What is the matter, sweetheart?" I asked, bending down to see if he was hurt. His shoulders sagged and his head was bent so low it almost touched the concrete. As another mournful moan escaped from deep in his throat, a tiny bird fell from his mouth to the floor. I gathered the stunned creature into my hands and stroked its smooth feathers. Smokey had handled it so gently that its greatest injury appeared to be only a bad case of fright.

Suddenly, the bird struggled in my cupped hands and I asked, "Do you want me to let the birdie go, Smokey?" But Smokey would not so much as even look up. I walked to the side door and opened my hands. The tiny bird looked at me for a fleeting moment and then flew happily into the early rays of the fresh morning sunlight.

I had never known Smokey to chase or stalk a bird, much less catch one. He liked to play with mice, dead or alive, but only after I caught them. And he wouldn't think of eating them. He liked to chase lizards and bugs, but never birds. This was so unlike him.

Single, however, was a different story. From the moment he could climb trees, he hunted birds. One late afternoon, we watched him determinedly chase a low-flying bird across our back deck. He swatted the bird, knocked it down on the deck, but the bird flew up again. This process was repeated across the long deck until they both came to the end of the deck where the bird took air again just over the steps that led down to the yard below. Single made one final lunge. Grabbing the bird with his front paws, and tucking his body into a ball, he rolled down the steps. When he landed on the grass below, he still held the bird securely to his chest. We watched him strut away proudly, carrying his tasty reward to a secret corner where he could enjoy it privately.

I walked back to Smokey, who sat dejectedly with head still bowed. "It's okay, sweetheart," I consoled him. "You didn't do anything wrong. It's completely natural for cats to chase birds, and to eat them. That's the way God made cats, so don't feel ashamed. However, just because it's natural, you don't have to do it if you don't want to." I sat on the edge of the platform curb and lifted Smokey into my lap. I stroked his soft fur, but he refused to look me in the face, preferring to tuck his head out of sight under my arm. "I know it's hard living with a wild and free spirit like Single, but don't compare yourself with him. You don't have to do what he does and he doesn't have to do what you want to do. The two of you are uniquely different, and I love you both."

As I continued to stroke him, I became aware of how much I needed this one-sided conversation. I was having my own struggles. I'd recently fallen into the habit of comparing myself to a multitalented, dynamic, gregarious woman at church who seemed to have an unending source of energy and talents. Why can't I be more like her? I had moaned mentally. Why can't I have half her energy? She accomplishes, I procrastinate. She excels, I daydream. She has talent, I have excuses. What's wrong with me? What's wrong with her? Like Smokey, I was beating myself up too. "I know how you feel, Smokey," I told him. "Next to that lady, I look like a lazy klutz! I feel so intimidated when I'm around her."

But then, right there in the shadow of all her outward perfection, I realized that God doesn't want me to be like anyone else. He just wants me to be me—and to be the best me that I can be with His help. He loves each of His children. And none of us are perfect, no matter how good we look to others.

Soothed, probably more by my dulcet tones than the wisdom of my theology, Smokey slowly lifted his head and looked into my face. He meowed softly, laid his head on my arm, and purred contentedly. As for the bird, I think it was pretty happy that Smokey's talents weren't in the bird-hunting department.

Remind me, heavenly Father, that because You created only one me, I am unique and have a special place to fill in eternity's plan. Help me to resist the temptation to try to fit myself into someone else's mold. May I allow You to mold me into exactly what You want me to be as I fulfill Your plan. Amen

I praise you because I am fearfully and wonderfully made; your works are wonderful, I know that full well. My frame was not hidden from you when I was made in the secret place. When I was woven together in the depths of the earth, your eyes saw my unformed body. All the days ordained for me were written in your book before one of them came to be.

PSALM 139:14-16 NIV

COULD THE PURR BE ANYTHING
BUT CONTEMPLATIVE?

IRVING TOWNSEND

THE REASON CATS CLIMB IS SO
THAT THEY CAN LOOK DOWN ON
ALMOST EVERY OTHER ANIMAL.
IT'S ALSO THE REASON THEY HATE BIRDS.

K. C. BUFFINGTON

THERE IS NOTHING IN THE ANIMAL
WORLD, TO MY MIND, MORE DELIGHTFUL
THAN GROWN CATS AT PLAY.
THEY ARE SO SWIFT AND LIGHT AND
GRACEFUL, SO SUBTLE AND DESIGNING,
AND YET SO RICHLY COMICAL.

MONICA EDWARDS

Garbage

Single was a well-fed cat. He received daily vitamins and the best in nutritious food formulated with his specific needs in mind. He enjoyed eating his meals and rarely left a morsel in his bowl. Yet many mornings I walked into the kitchen and caught him with a paw deep in the disposal, up to his shoulder, digging around for garbage. On the counter lay stringy pieces of gristle, shredded celery stalks, and remnants of unidentifiable matter. Sometimes he gagged on some contraband and coughed it up. He usually avoided that type of substance thereafter. Usually.

I wondered why he would go fishing around in the garbage disposal for things that are not fit for cat consumption, being so well fed? And why would we sometimes do the same? Not in the garbage disposals of our kitchens, but in the garbage disposals of life.

We are well fed on the Word, downright fat with scriptural knowledge, yet we sometimes experience a sudden urge to go digging through the world's muck and rubbish just to see what we can find. We don't know what we are looking for, but we wonder if maybe we're missing something that might be pleasing to our taste, something not in our regular diet. So we chew on things not fit for Christian consumption. If we are fortunate we will get sick, throw it up, and give it up. If not, we may continue sampling until we develop a taste, or even a dependency or craving, for something that damages our mental health and spiritual vitality. Even with the help of the Great Physician, our recovery could be painfully slow. We'd all be a lot better off if we'd just remember to keep our paws out of the garbage.

Father, give me wisdom to decline
when the world passes its tray of
attractively arranged contraband. And
should I be foolish enough to sample
any of it, may I spit it out quickly
before it becomes so big in my life
that it chews me up and spits me out
instead. Garbage is not on Your menu.
Amen

*That is why many among you are weak
and sick, and a number of you have fallen asleep.*

1 CORINTHIANS 11:30 NIV

THE CAT WHO DOESN'T ACT FINICKY
SOON LOSES CONTROL OF HIS OWNER.

MORRIS THE CAT

I HAVE NOTICED THAT WHAT CATS
MOST APPRECIATE IN A HUMAN BEING
IS NOT THE ABILITY TO PRODUCE FOOD
WHICH THEY TAKE FOR GRANTED—
BUT HIS OR HER ENTERTAINMENT VALUE.

GEOFFREY HOUSEHOLD

Hugged

I don't recall why my heart was so heavy that morning. Single, never far from me, lay dozing across the room, oblivious to my distress. Something had burdened me so deeply that I fell to my knees in prayer. With my face nestled in the cushion of my office chair, I sobbed out my pain to God. In my desolation, I recall crying out, "Oh, Lord, how I need You. If only You could reach down and hug me." In frustration I added, "You are all powerful. You can do anything. Can't You do this, just once?"

As I knelt, I felt Single's small feet begin walking up my sloped back. *Not now,* I thought, *I don't have time for games! I'm praying. As much as I love you, it's the Lord I need now.* But Single kept on walking. After reaching my shoulders, he lay down. With his warm body flattened against my back, he encircled my neck with his front paws, and purred softly in my ear as he lay there hugging me.

Father, I don't recall the reason for my prayer that day, but may I never forget Your response. Thank You for always being there when I need You the most, and for sending Your hug through the paws of one of Your creation. Amen

In the multitude of my anxieties within me,
Your comforts delight my soul.

PSALM 94:19 NKJV

THERE IS SOMETHING ABOUT THE
PRESENCE OF A CAT . . . THAT SEEMS TO
TAKE THE BITE OUT OF BEING ALONE.

LOUIS J. CAMUTI, D.V.M.

HAPPINESS IS LIKE A CAT.
IF YOU TRY TO COAX IT OR
CALL IT, IT WILL AVOID YOU;
IT WILL NEVER COME. BUT IF YOU
PAY NO ATTENTION TO IT AND GO
ABOUT YOUR BUSINESS, YOU'LL
FIND IT RUBBING AGAINST YOUR LEGS
AND JUMPING INTO YOUR LAP.

WILLIAM JOHN BENNETT

EVERYTHING A CAT IS AND DOES
PHYSICALLY IS TO ME BEAUTIFUL,
LOVELY, STIMULATING, SOOTHING,
ATTRACTIVE, AND AN ENCHANTMENT.

PAUL GALLICO

Only a Cat?

Heartbroken, I dragged myself to work that morning. How would I get through the day? My beloved Single was gone.

The day had dawned with the beauty of fresh air, sunshine, and birds singing. I stepped out on to our vine-covered balcony to let the beauty of the Ojai Valley sink in. As I stretched, I looked at the street below and saw Single lying there. "Single, you brat!" I called affectionately. "Get out of that street! You want to get hit by a car?" No response. Fingers of fear grabbed me as I noticed he was lying prone, with the side of his head on the pavement.

"No! Oh, no!" I cried as a huge hole ripped into my heart. Jerry rushed to the balcony as I fled down the outside stairs, and I heard him plead, "Honey, don't go down there!"

Pain engulfed me as I gently lifted Single's stiff body and held it to my breast. Standing there sobbing in the silent street, I felt Jerry's arms surround me and lead me back into the yard. For a long time, I held Single close to me and wept. At Jerry's gentle nudge, I kissed Single goodbye and released him to my husband's trembling hands.

While I prepared for a day that had suddenly betrayed me by turning cold and gray, Jerry laid Single in a grave.

Tears blurred his vision as he tapped a stick cross into the sod beneath spreading branches of the ancient white oak tree that Single had loved so dearly.

"Honey, don't go to work," Jerry said.

"I have to. With so few of us in the doctor's office today, I am really needed."

Numbed by pain, I went through the motions until a coworker asked me what was wrong. Tears escaped as I briefly explained the cause of my quiet pain. For a moment, she gazed at my swollen face and reddened eyes then she softly said, "But . . . it's only a cat."

Only a cat? I rushed to the restroom where my tears flowed freely in private. *Lord, I'm not going to make it through this day without Your help,* I prayed silently. *I don't expect to go through life without pain, but I just ask that You not let me hurt so much. I've experienced pain before over lost pets but never anything like this. Will You take away just some of the pain so I can bear it?* Gently, a warm peace came over me. I regained my composure and returned to my work routine.

During those moments when I wasn't consumed with office pressures, my pain returned, but not as intensely as before. *Probably because I'm so busy,* I thought.

It was unusually hectic at work, and by the time I arrived at home I was fatigued and weary, ready to succumb to the terrible pain that had led me into the day. But it never came. The pain seemed to go only so far and then mysteriously stop, as though held back by an unseen boundary. It's not that there was no pain, it's just that there was a definite line of demarcation that prevented it from going beyond a certain point, like a golden cord that would not let it pass. *How strange,* I thought.

Then I recalled my prayer. It was obvious that God had answered it. He knew my pain was not because of the loss of "only a cat," but because of the wrenching from me of something very special, a piece of my heart that left a painful void. He, who would not let the fall of a sparrow go unnoticed, had noted my pain.

This answered prayer provided more than I had asked—a tiny window through which I could see an even greater principle at work. Because God was deeply touched by my pain due to the loss of "only a cat," would He not also help me with even greater pains flung upon me by the storms of life?

Thank You, Father, for answered prayer.
Thank You for the assurance that I can
face the future without fear of being
destroyed by pain. Amen

You have turned for me my mourning into
dancing; You have put off my sackcloth
and clothed me with gladness, to the end
that my glory may sing praise to You and
not be silent. O LORD my God,
I will give thanks to You forever.

PSALM 30:11-12 NKJV

NO AMOUNT OF TIME CAN ERASE
THE MEMORY OF A GOOD CAT,
AND NO AMOUNT OF MASKING TAPE
CAN EVER TOTALLY REMOVE HIS FUR
FROM YOUR COUCH.

LEO DWORKEN

MY CAT KNOWS THE SONG IN MY HEART
AND PURRS IT TO ME WHEN MY MEMORY FAILS.

ANONYMOUS

O HEAVEN WILL NOT EVER HEAVEN BE
UNLESS MY CATS ARE THERE TO WELCOME ME.

EPITAPH IN A PET CEMETERY

Healthy Eating

Skeeter is a cat who belongs to my sister, Chris. Because he is easily influenced by the eating habits of others, Skeeter has little discretion regarding his dietary intake. He thinks that whatever he sees humans eat, he should also eat.

Chris once encountered Skeeter as he was downing the last of her morning vitamins—a huge garlic capsule. The other cats didn't get close to him for a week! Because he ignores the verbal "no trespassing" messages regarding the kitchen counter and table, all food is stored out of sight.

One of Skeeter's favorite dishes is cooked broccoli. He is so excited by the first whiff of this, his favorite treat, that Chris has to remove a portion from the pan prematurely to give to him. Overcome with excitement (if only kids were this enthusiastic over vegetables!), he dances impatiently on his hind feet as she blows on the broccoli for cooling. This practice has led Skeeter to the erroneous conclusion that whatever is blown upon must taste good. Consequently, matches, candles, and such must be carefully hidden in order to keep Skeeter from consuming things that were never meant to be eaten by a cat.

That reminds me a little of us. We watch what others are eating and want to sample the same things. We get caught up in the world's sales pitches and jump to the false conclusion that because "everyone else is doing it" we should do it also.

It has been said that we should chew what we eat at least thirty-three times before we swallow. But some things should never be sampled in the first place—much less chewed up and swallowed.

Father, teach me moral and spiritual discernment. Give me wisdom to realize that what is swallowed by others may not be fit for consumption by Your children. Amen

Teach me good judgment and knowledge,
for I believe Your commandments.

PSALM 119:66 NKJV

YOU OWN A DOG BUT YOU FEED A CAT.

JENNY DE VRIES

A CAT SEES US AS THE DOG.
A CAT SEES HIMSELF AS THE HUMAN.

ANONYMOUS

IF YOU PUT DOWN FOOD AND THE CAT EATS,
IT'S HUNGRY. IF IT DOESN'T, IT ISN'T.

LARRY MADRID

The Purr-fect Position

Chris's other cat, Taz (short for Tasmania), had been sick for several days. The vet suspected that the cat had a virus. Chris carefully followed all the instructions, but one night, two weeks later, it was apparent that Taz was extremely ill. Fearful that he would die in her arms, Chris frantically paged the vet at 6 AM and she was instructed to take Taz to the animal hospital as soon as possible.

After careful examination, the doctor suspected a blockage and ordered the necessary tests. Aware of her exhaustion, he encouraged Chris to go home and go to bed, promising to call her with the results. There was nothing she could do now anyway.

Back at her house, fatigued and broken in heart and spirit, Chris fell to her knees. Sobbing, she cried out to her heavenly Father for help. "Lord, I've done all I can. You know how much I love Taz and it breaks my heart to think of him dying. I know he's only a small animal and some people may think he's not that important in the scheme of things, but he must be important to You for You created him. Surely You would not want him to suffer. Will You please help?" She fell asleep praying.

When she awoke, the words *corn cob* flashed in her mind and would not go away. Could it be? Just prior to Taz getting sick, Chris recalled she had served corn on the cob for dinner. Taz liked corn, it was one of his favorite treats. Could he have retrieved a cob from the garbage? Did he eat part of the cob and that was the obstruction? Minutes later, she rushed into the hospital room where the doctor was working with Taz.

After relating her suspicions to him, he replied, "We will need to open him up." Chris agreed.

As the doctor's skilled fingers probed the stomach of sleeping Taz, he felt a foreign object. Upon retrieval, it was found, indeed, to be a small piece of corn cob.

Taz regained his health and is now living evidence of answered prayer, thanks to the skillful hands of his surgeon and the Creator who cared.

"I was so busy trying to solve the problem all by myself that I didn't take time to ask for help from the One who has all the answers," Chris said later. "Not until all of my efforts had failed did I finally fully rely on God for help. And when I did, He answered my prayers."

Sometimes it's not just pieces of corn cob that can become obstructive. Our self-reliance can block us too.

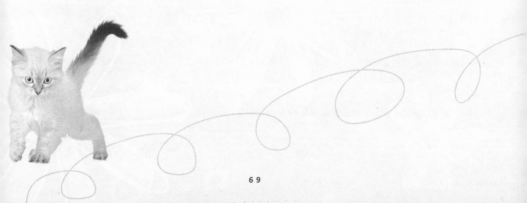

Lord, let me not come to You as a last resort, but as a first stop. And remind me that the best position I can be in, when I need Your help, is in the position of trust. Amen

In my distress I called upon the LORD.
. . . He heard my voice.

PSALM 18:6 NKJV

EVERYTHING I KNOW I LEARNED
FROM MY CAT: WHEN YOU'RE HUNGRY, EAT.
WHEN YOU'RE TIRED, NAP IN A SUNBEAM.
WHEN YOU GO TO THE VET'S, PEE ON YOUR OWNER.

GARY SMITH

CATS ARE RATHER DELICATE CREATURES
AND THEY ARE SUBJECT TO A GOOD MANY
AILMENTS, BUT I NEVER HEARD OF ONE
WHO SUFFERED FROM INSOMNIA.

JOSEPH WOOD KRUTCH

A LITTLE LION, SMALL AND DAINTY
SWEET WITH SEA-GREY EYES
AND SOFTLY STEPPING FEET.

GRAHAM TOMSON

Letting Go

Wearily, I drove home from work. It had been a long, hard day and I looked forward to a relaxing evening with Jerry and Smokey. Following Single's death weeks earlier, Smokey sought more attention from us—attention that Jerry and I were eager to give, because it helped us deal with our loss, also.

As I glanced through the sliding glass door to the backyard, I saw Jerry walking toward the house with a shovel in his hand. My heart froze. The last time I saw that scene it had followed Single's death. Oh no, it couldn't be!

With pale face, Jerry took me into his arms and said, "Honey, I'm so sorry. I just finished burying Smokey."

Stunned, I asked, "What happened?"

There was a long pause before he answered. "Honey, this is going to hurt."

Hurt! How can it hurt any more than what I just went through with Single's death? I wondered. "What do you mean?"

Taking a deep breath, he answered slowly, "Smokey was killed by a vicious dog late this afternoon."

There was a leash law in our town, somewhat enforced, but I had noticed no packs of dogs roaming our streets. In our quiet community, I rarely saw a dog unleashed.

"I don't understand. How did it happen?"

He explained that when our neighbor glanced out her upstairs window from across the street, she noticed a big black dog stop at the end of our walk. She saw Smokey, asleep in his usual place near the front door, partially hidden from view of the street. As she watched, the dog turned and suddenly raced up the walk. Before Smokey could fully awaken, the dog grabbed him by the throat.

The neighbor ran from her house, screaming at the dog as she crossed the street, but he would not release his hold on Smokey. She picked up a big stick and charged him. He dropped Smokey and, snarling through bared teeth, advanced toward her. As she retreated, the dog returned to a stunned Smokey whose valiant battle was no match for the powerful jaws of his predator. Horror gripped me as I imagined the terror and pain experienced by our gentle pet.

Our neighbor rode with Jerry in his truck for several evenings following the tragedy in search of the dog. The third evening, she suddenly yelled, "That's him!" pointing to a large black dog ambling alone down the street. They followed him to his house where the owner was apprised of the situation and agreed to secure the dog. Jerry drove by a week later and saw that the dog was chained up in the backyard as the owner had promised.

Having completed the task of seeing that the dog was located and indeed confined, Jerry let go of his rage. But I was still angry—angry at the dog, angry at its owners, angry at the city for not enforcing its leash laws, angry that animal control hadn't come and helped when our neighbor had called, angry because our Smokey was gone and, most of all, angered by my tortured visions of Smokey's terrifying death. Somebody should pay! But who? And how?

Consumed with my grief and pain, I repeated and relived the story over and over to anyone who would listen. Yes, the dog was chained now, but so was I by my anger and bitterness.

I went to God in prayer for help, but He would not cooperate. He refused to send massive boils to the dog's body and make him die a slow death as punishment. He also refused to make the dog's owners have flat tires on all their vehicles and boll weevils eat their landscaping. Finally, I gave up. "I am so miserable, Lord," I pleaded, "please take this anger from me." But it still remained.

I went to God's Word for solace. Each time I opened the Bible, my gaze fell on God's instructions to forgive. There was a pattern—no coincidence—but my heart rebelled at what I read, and my thoughts challenged the truths God kept before me.

"What is this, Lord? I'm supposed to forgive a dog! Give me a break! I'll forgive him when he sits up and begs for it!" But I knew it wasn't just the dog. "I don't want to forgive that dog, his owner, or anybody responsible for my pet's death!" I said aloud to God. "I want somebody to pay! I'd like to shoot that dog! Maybe not kill him, but shoot all his teeth out. Then he certainly wouldn't hurt any other helpless animals, and then his owners would know how I feel!"

"Sweetheart," Jerry said one day, "you've got to let it go. You're not that good of a shot. And anyway, nothing is going to bring Smokey back. Your anger is only making you miserable, as well as those around you."

I knew what he said was true. I finally went to God in honesty for help. "Father, I feel like I don't want to forgive, but I do want to do what You want me to do. So, would You please help me to want to forgive?"

I don't know when it happened, but one day I realized I was free. I had forgiven everyone and everything involved with Smokey's death. Peace had replaced my rebellion.

Yes, Smokey was gone, but his beautiful memories had returned—freed when I let go of my bitterness.

Heavenly Father, thank You for understanding when I feel like I don't want to forgive. Help me to let go of my hurts more quickly in the future, so I won't suffer so long and so that You will forgive me of my trespasses. Amen

If you forgive others for their sins,
your Father in heaven will also
forgive you for your sins.
MATTHEW 6:14 NCV

UNTIL ONE HAS LOVED AN ANIMAL,
A PART OF ONE'S SOUL REMAINS UNAWAKENED.

ANATOLE FRANCE

IN THE BEGINNING,
GOD CREATED MAN,
BUT SEEING HIM SO FEEBLE,
HE GAVE HIM THE CAT.

WARREN ECKSTEIN

WHO CAN BELIEVE THAT THERE
IS NO SOUL BEHIND THOSE LUMINOUS EYES!

THEOPHILE GAUTIER

A Place for Gato

"Are you sure we are ready for another cat?" I asked Jerry. "Our hearts haven't yet healed from the loss of Smokey and Single."

"Well, I don't know. All I know is that I told Rose we would pray about adopting her cat. She and Steve are moving to a new location that won't allow pets."

"Don't they know anyone else who could take him? Besides, we've always gotten kittens before. We've never taken a grown cat. I'd miss all those cute antics."

Rose was Jerry's secretary. He had found her crying at her desk one day and learned that she and her husband Steve would have to give up their beloved Gato. Her response had been a tearful one. "I know God has the perfect place for him, but I don't know of anyone else on earth I would want as a mommy and daddy for my Gato. All I ask is that you guys just pray about it."

"I told her I couldn't make any promises, but that we would pray about it," Jerry replied defensively.

"Then, that is what we will do. I'll discuss it with Tamara and we will all pray about it." When Tamara came in we talked it over. We reviewed Gato's description as related to Jerry by Rose. He was a large, black, long-haired, one-year-old-going-on-two neutered male with a white chest and white feet. His name was El Gato Gordo, "the fat cat" in Spanish. We discussed all the advantages and disadvantages of getting a grown cat. We prayed about it, and I left the matter in Tamara's hands since she would be spending more time with him. "Take your time," I said.

Later that evening, Tamara came downstairs and announced to me, "I've been praying and thinking about it a lot, and I think we should take Gato."

I was mildly surprised at how quickly she had decided. I halfway expected (and wanted) her to opt for a kitten.

A couple of weeks later, Steve, with Gato in his arms and a tearful Rose beside him, appeared at our door. Once inside, I asked if Gato would let me hold him. Steve responded, "I don't know, he doesn't usually take to strangers, but we can try."

With no trace of resistance, Gato allowed me to gather him into my arms, where he immediately relaxed. It was as though God had whispered to him, "Don't be afraid, this is your new home."

Yes, God does answer prayer regardless of the need. And He had the perfect place for Gato—in our hearts and home. For almost fifteen years.

Father, thank You for caring about the concerns of your children. You blend the prolonged prayers of the heavy-hearted with quickly and lightly offered prayers, and produce perfect blessings for all involved. Amen

Even though you are bad, you know
how to give good gifts to your children.
How much more your heavenly Father
will give good things to those who ask him!

MATTHEW 7:11 NCV

OUR PERFECT COMPANIONS NEVER
HAVE FEWER THAN FOUR FEET.

COLETTE

MANY CATS SIMPLY POUNCE
TO THEIR OWN DRUMMERS.

KAREN DUPREY

IF YOU WOULD KNOW WHAT A CAT
IS THINKING ABOUT, YOU MUST HOLD
ITS PAW IN YOUR HAND FOR A LONG TIME.

JULES CHAMPFLEURY

Exposé

How I envy Gato! He is so at ease with people. One night he sauntered into the middle of my husband's surprise fiftieth birthday celebration. In the presence of thirty people, mostly strangers to him, he lay down in the middle of the floor and, with belly exposed, took a nap.

There are days when I wish I could take a nap so easily! I am told that an animal displays trust when it exposes its belly—an open and vulnerable position.

I wish I could be more like Gato. Too often I am on guard, afraid to expose the real me. I hide behind façades because I fear rejection, that someone might think unkind thoughts about me or, worse yet, take a verbal swat at me.

And yet, who are the people I admire most? Those who expose their softness. Those who are open and transparent, comfortable and at peace with who they are. Those whose identity always appears to remain intact even when someone treats them badly.

That sounds a lot like Jesus. Jesus knew who He was—the Great Physician and Savior—and why He was here. He was secure in His identity, even when others rejected Him. He was at ease among strangers and unfamiliar circumstances. He never feared the verbal swipes, threats, or rejection of the religious leaders. He selflessly loved them (and us) all the way to the cross.

Maybe if I concentrated on accepting and respecting myself for who I am (a daughter of the King) and focus more on why I am here (to honor Him), I could ignore the expectations I imagine others have of me. I could then expose my real self and, like Gato, lose no sleep over what people might think. I could lie back comfortably in His arms, fully trusting His care.

Holy Spirit, help me to accept others for who they are, just as Jesus did. Teach me to give them unconditional love and respect because I know who I am—a child of the King. Amen

God began doing a good work in you,
and I am sure he will continue it until it is
finished when Jesus Christ comes again.
PHILIPPIANS 1:6 NCV

CAT'S MOTTO: NO MATTER WHAT
YOU'VE DONE WRONG, ALWAYS TRY TO
MAKE IT LOOK LIKE THE DOG DID IT.

ANONYMOUS

EVERYTHING COMES TO THOSE
WHO WAIT . . . EXCEPT A CAT.

MARILYN PETERSON

ALL CATS LOVE A CUSHIONED COUCH.

THEOCRITES

Fear

There is a distinct scar, two-and-a-half inches long, on the underside of my left forearm. While preparing to leave for his office one morning, Jerry and I discussed our day's plans. Gato purred softly in my arms as I gently stroked his fur. When Jerry turned on the blow dryer, Gato panicked and slashed my arm as he bolted for freedom. The cut was deep and the wound bled profusely. It required no stitches, but now, almost twenty years later, the fine curved scar is still visible.

Later that day, after inquiring about my bandaged arm, a friend remarked, "That would be one dead cat if it were mine!"

Cat lovers recoil at such a statement, because it is obvious Gato reacted from fright. Fear caused him to lash out, an instinctive response to protect himself from what he perceived to be a threat.

I hope my scar never goes away. It reminds me that friends also can lash out in sudden retaliation when they feel frightened or threatened, and cut me deeply. This reaction may be brought about more by what is going on within their minds than from any real infraction on my part.

The Bible says, "A friend loves at all times" (Proverbs 17:17). And since I am a friend lover as well as a cat lover, may I never yield to the temptation to kill the friendship over an unintentional wound or a self-defensive swipe.

Lord, help me to understand and be patient when friends lash out at me through misunderstandings. Teach me to be as faithful a friend to others as You are to me. Amen

Faithful are the wounds of a friend,
But the kisses of an enemy are deceitful.
PROVERBS 27:6 NKJV

CATS KNOW HOW TO OBTAIN
FOOD WITHOUT LABOR,
SHELTER WITHOUT CONFINEMENT,
AND LOVE WITHOUT PENALTIES.

W. L. GEORGE

IT IS IMPOSSIBLE FOR A LOVER OF CATS
TO BANISH THESE ALERT, GENTLE,
AND DISCRIMINATING FRIENDS,
WHO GIVE US JUST ENOUGH OF THEIR
REGARD AND COMPLAISANCE
TO MAKE US HUNGER FOR MORE.

AGNES REPPLIER

WHAT GREATER GIFT
THAN THE LOVE OF A CAT?

CHARLES DICKENS

Gato's Problem

Gato had a problem. He didn't like the taste of his new food. He wanted his former food with its familiar flavor. He didn't care about the nutritional value or mineral levels—just give him the taste he wanted and he would be happy.

Because of his predisposition to kidney stones, the vet had put Gato on a special diet. I was told to check the ingredients and percentage levels of certain minerals before buying his food. And that wasn't a problem. The nutritious foods he needed were readily available. The only problem was Gato's taste.

There were frustrating battles of the will. He rebelled and would turn his nose up at the healthier new food I offered. I refused to yield and kept setting out fresh bowls of the doctor-recommended cuisine.

"He will either eat when he gets hungry enough," I declared to my family who had all taken his side, "or he will starve!" They were convinced he would starve. I was convinced I could wear him down before things got too ugly.

Gato tried many tactics to force the issue. First, he sat motionless in protest by his bowl for prolonged periods of time. I ignored him.

Then, he tried the silent treatment. He ignored me, pretending I was invisible, especially when I called him to dinner. I ignored his ignorings.

Next, he tried the guilt-trip tactic. He picked at his food and made gagging noises. I paid no attention. My kids had tried the same tactic plenty of times whenever I served a dish they didn't like.

Finally, Gato tried retaliation. He ate part of his food, walked into the living room, and threw it up on the carpet. A little dramatic, but still I didn't relent.

I tried different flavors so he had a lot of choices. It's just that none of his choices included the bad foods he craved. I did everything in my power to help him like the prescribed diet, but he had to do his part too.

At last, to the family's surprise, he came around. Once he began eating the food he had tried so hard to avoid, he cultivated a taste for it and started begging for more. I couldn't keep enough of it in the house.

On his new diet he enjoyed benefits far greater than merely avoiding kidney stones. He was rarely sick, got into fewer fights, had boundless energy, and played like a kitten—at eleven years of age! And the two of us became very close again as he followed my every footstep. All because he was feeding on healthier fare.

I, too, once needed the prescribed treatment for my problem—the terminal disease of sin. Left unchecked, it would have resulted in eternal separation from all that is good. God offered me an antidote, a new and special diet, researched, formulated, and paid for by His Son. I rebelled at first, walking away from the healthier life of unconditional love and forgiveness, but eventually I accepted it. And I am now feeling so much better and walking so much closer to Him as I daily try to follow in His steps.

Heavenly Father, thank You for
providing the perfect diet for my eternal
nutrition. And, thank You, Jesus, for
paying for it. Amen

How sweet are Your words to my taste,
Sweeter than honey to my mouth!

PSALM 119:103 NKJV

ANYONE WHO CLAIMS THAT A CAT
CANNOT GIVE A DIRTY LOOK EITHER
HAS NEVER KEPT A CAT OR IS
SINGULARLY UNOBSERVANT.

MAURICE BURTON

THE CAT IS, ABOVE ALL THINGS, A DRAMATIST.

MARGARET BENSON

CATS HAVE ENORMOUS PATIENCE WITH THE
LIMITATIONS OF THE HUMAN MIND.
THEY REALIZE . . . THAT WE HAVE AN
INFURIATING INABILITY TO UNDERSTAND,
LET ALONE FOLLOW, EVEN THE SIMPLEST
AND MOST EXPLICIT OF DIRECTIONS.

CLEVELAND AMORY

Praise?

Gato quickly learned to stand on his hind feet, lift his two front paws high above his head, and move them up and down as a "praise the Lord" gesture for his food. Although the depth of his gratitude was questionable, he usually was anxious to do this because he knew he would be fed immediately afterward. Sometimes, however, he was reluctant. Especially when he got a whiff of his food and realized it was not one of his favorites. Not only did he not want to praise the Lord in thanks, but he acted downright ungrateful.

Sometimes God sets before me a plate of circumstances for which I do not feel thankful. I prefer to walk away from them. Why should I give thanks to God, much less praise Him?

I am learning, however, that when I am ungrateful, my attitude develops a negative taste that looks for the unpleasant things in life. And it always finds them. When my heart is grateful, it develops an attitude of praise regardless of the distasteful circumstances. It then feasts upon the riches from God's table of truth—tasty morsels that validate the reality that God loves me and is always in control. And that is certainly a delicious fact worthy of praise! In fact, that's enough to get Gato raising his paws in praise too!

Heavenly Father, thank You for what
You set before Me. Give Me discernment
in developing My tastes. May My
appetite for gratitude be whetted and
My hunger filled with praise for the
Bread of Life all of My days. Amen

Give thanks whatever happens.
That is what God wants for you in Christ Jesus.

1 THESSALONIANS 5:18 NCV

BLESS THEIR LITTLE POINTED FACES
AND THEIR BIG, LOYAL, LOVING HEARTS.
IF A CAT DID NOT PUT A FIRM PAW DOWN
NOW AND THEN, HOW COULD
HIS HUMAN REMAIN POSSESSED?

WINIFRED CARRIERE

A CAT'S PURR IS THE SOUND
OF IT GENERATING CUTE.

ANONYMOUS

PURRING BESIDE OUR FIREPLACES
AND PATTERING ALONG OUR BACK FENCES,
WE HAVE GOT A WILD BEAST AS UNCOWED
AND UNCORRUPTED AS ANY UNDER HEAVEN.

ALAN DEVOE

Vive La Différence!

Divon observed Gato with interest when he "praised the Lord" for his food. Divon was a guest cat, owned by our adult daughter, Tamara, who was staying with us while recuperating from an illness.

Taking advantage of Divon's interest, I taught her to stand on her hind legs in a begging posture for her food, but she never felt inclined to wave her paws in praise as Gato did.

One evening when guests were in our home, Gato ambled in and announced he was ready for dinner. As they watched, Jerry ran him through his "praise-the-Lord-before-eating" routine. With a twinkle in his eye, Jerry joked proudly, "Gato is a Christian cat."

At that moment, Divon entered the room, and Jerry added, "Divon, however, is not a Christian cat. She refuses to praise the Lord for her food."

Overhearing this from the hall, Tamara countered loudly, "Divon is too a Christian cat! She's just not charismatic!"

How many of us are of the opinion that other worshipers of Christ aren't really Christians if they don't worship the same way we do? The truth is, not all of us enjoy waving our arms in praise. Those of us who do can't imagine ever sitting quietly as the heart overflows with gratitude and praise. Some of us do both some of the time. Many of us, unfortunately, rarely do either any of the time. We are too busy doing religious activities instead of worshiping the One we're serving. However we feel most comfortable in worshiping our Lord, like Gato or like Divon, I'm certain every heart is grateful for its place at the spiritual table where the Bread of Life is the main course.

Heavenly Father, remind me that regardless of how we express ourselves to You, quietly or loudly, we belong to the same family. And the praise that pleases You most comes from the life that resembles Your Son. Amen

Because your love is better than life,
my lips will glorify you.
I will praise you as long as I live,
and in your name I will lift up my hands.

PSALM 63:3-4 NIV

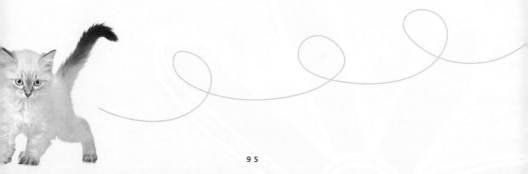

CATS AS A CLASS HAVE NEVER
COMPLETELY GOT OVER THE
SNOOTINESS CAUSED BY THE FACT
THAT IN ANCIENT EGYPT THEY
WERE WORSHIPPED AS GODS.

P. G. WODEHOUSE

FOR A MAN TO TRULY
UNDERSTAND REJECTION, HE
MUST FIRST BE IGNORED BY A CAT.

ANONYMOUS

THERE ARE PEOPLE WHO RESHAPE
THE WORLD BY FORCE OR ARGUMENT,
BUT THE CAT JUST LIES THERE, DOZING,
AND THE WORLD QUIETLY RESHAPES
ITSELF TO SUIT HIS COMFORT
AND CONVENIENCE.

ALLEN AND IVY DODD

Two-Faced

From the moment our granddaughter Bailey began to crawl, Gato's goal in life was to avoid her. As soon as he heard Bailey at the front door, he disappeared. This became worrisome to Bailey when she was around three years old, so she asked, "Why doesn't Gato like me?"

I explained that it was not that he didn't like her; he was just uncomfortable around her. "He may have been mistreated at some time by little kids who are not as kind as you. When you get bigger he'll let you pet him," I promised.

Just before her fifth birthday, Bailey took Gato his food bowl and he allowed her to stroke him several times as he ate. She suddenly turned to me from across the room and exclaimed, "Grandma Kitty, Gato likes me! He finally likes me! He let me pet him and he didn't run away. I must be big now!" Her face beamed with pleasure.

As her joyful chatter continued about her long-awaited acceptance, I saw Gato walk up and stop just behind her. He looked up at her for a long lingering moment. Suddenly, he hissed several times and walked on past. She didn't see or hear what he did behind her back, but I did.

I am reminded of this scene when I am tempted to merely tolerate certain people. I don't want to give them a chance to get close to me. Although I have no desire to get to know them and to love them for who they are, I appear to be nothing but sweetness and kindness to their face while I hiss behind their back. They never know it, but God sees the entire scene. He doesn't just see the first face, but the second face too.

Father, please forgive me when I barricade myself behind a plastic smile and deny others the opportunity of friendship. Teach me to be open and accessible to them, as You are to me. Amen

He who works deceit shall not dwell within my house;
He who tells lies shall not continue in my presence.

PSALM 101:7 NKJV

A CAT HAS ABSOLUTE
EMOTIONAL HONESTY.
HUMAN BEINGS, FOR ONE
REASON OR ANOTHER,
MAY HIDE THEIR FEELINGS,
BUT A CAT DOES NOT.

ERNEST HEMINGWAY

IF ANIMALS COULD SPEAK,
THE DOG WOULD BE A
BLUNDERING OUTSPOKEN FELLOW;
BUT THE CAT WOULD HAVE
THE RARE GRACE OF NEVER
SAYING A WORD TOO MUCH.

MARK TWAIN

OUR CHARACTER IS WHAT GOD
AND CATS KNOW OF US.

THOMAS PAINE

CATS ARE DESIGNATED FRIENDS.

NORMAN CORWIN

My Territory!

I was headed for the front door to take out table scraps for the fox bowl when Gato walked into the hall. *Oh, rats!* I thought. I didn't want him to follow me outside and possibly become involved with the wild fox. As I slowly opened the door, I noted a feral cat sitting on the railing of the deck. I quickly extended my leg as a barrier to keep Gato from seeing the cat and running outside. Too late! He saw the other cat and reacted in territorial anger, viciously attacking my leg. Huge red stains suddenly appeared through my thick ski socks worn over the bottom of my sweats. As the puncture wounds bled profusely, anger flared within me at his reaction.

While bandaging my leg, my anger lessened as I recalled past outbursts of my own. One in particular. An innocent friend had been hurt when I lashed out irresponsibly toward another whom I felt was in my space. Territorial anger had clouded my vision just as it had Gato's, and the one nearest me had been wounded because of my retaliation.

I glanced at Gato who sat subdued in his corner, and said, "I forgive you, Gato, just as my friends forgave me."

Holy Spirit, thank You for nudging me about my failures. May they come to mind quickly when I am faced with the need to forgive others. And, Lord, thank You for forgiving me of my transgressions. Amen

If you don't forgive others, your Father in heaven will not forgive your sins.

MATTHEW 6:15 NCV

THOSE WHO WILL PLAY WITH CATS
MUST EXPECT TO BE SCRATCHED.

CERVANTES

SOME PEOPLE SAY MAN IS
THE MOST DANGEROUS
ANIMAL ON THE PLANET.
OBVIOUSLY THOSE PEOPLE HAVE
NEVER MET AN ANGRY CAT.

LILLIAN JOHNSON

IF THE CLAWS DIDN'T RETRACT,
CATS WOULD BE LIKE VELCRO.

DR. BRUCE FOGLE

Listen!

For his safety, I would call Gato in at night. We lived in a rural area of secluded woods that harbored bobcats, skunks, raccoons, and coyotes. Most of the time, he answered with his soft whir response as he bounded up the steps.

But, sometimes, when the moon was full, exciting, strange sounds and smells filled the air, and he did not want to come in. I'd wait a little longer and call again. I was patient, for I understood the stirrings of his heart.

Sometimes, despite my persistent calls, there was no response. The only sounds I heard were those of crickets and the calls of the hoot owls.

I'd go into the darkness and look for him as I called his name. I knew that he was there. And I knew that he knew that I knew he was there. But he would be silent, waiting for me to pass by. When I'd find him, he was usually on the verge of getting into trouble. Yet he allowed me to gently pick him up and bring him in to safety.

Sometimes we don't respond when God calls us. We know that He is calling, and He knows that we know. But we quietly ignore Him, waiting for Him to pass by. The world's exciting sounds—things that can cause us pain—call to us and lure us. If we're smart, we'll respond to His call quickly before we get into trouble, trouble that we may not even realize is out there.

Father, when Your Holy Spirit comes looking for me and I am on the verge of making a decision that could bring me harm, give me wisdom to listen and respond. And please, Father, please don't ever stop calling me. Amen

Listen closely to what I tell you;
listen carefully to what I say.

ISAIAH 28:23 NCV

NIGHT WILL ALWAYS REMAIN
A CAT'S MAGICAL, FANCIFUL TIME.

JERRY CLIMER

A CAT DETERMINED NOT TO BE
FOUND CAN FOLD ITSELF UP LIKE
A POCKET HANDKERCHIEF
IF IT WANTS TO.

LOUIS J. CAMUTI, D.V.M.

THE CAT HAS ALWAYS BEEN ASSOCIATED
WITH THE MOON. LIKE THE MOON IT
COMES TO LIFE AT NIGHT, ESCAPING FROM
HUMANITY AND WANDERING OVER HOUSETOPS
WITH ITS EYES BEAMING OUT THROUGH THE DARKNESS.

PATRICIA DALE-GREEN

No Search and Rescue

"Gato! This is my last call! I am much too tired to run around in the woods looking for you tonight!" More "last calls" followed, but still no response. I tried to ignore the twinge of guilt as I fell into bed, exhausted.

I should have called him in before dark, like I usually do. *But maybe he will be okay this one time,* I thought wearily. *I worry too much.*

The next morning, I found our pet huddled on the upstairs deck by my bedroom door—scratched, cut, bruised, and frightened. I picked him up and wept as I held him closely. "I'm so sorry, Gato."

After making certain that there were no broken bones and his scratches and cuts were minor, I offered him breakfast. He was too exhausted to eat. He drank a little water, then limped to his pallet where he slept soundly all day.

I vowed I would never again let him stay out all night, no matter how tired I was! He must have made his own vow, too, for several full moons passed before he ignored my call again.

Unlike Gato's owner, our heavenly Father is never too tired to search for us, nor will He give up. He will keep calling. And He will keep looking. No matter how dark the night or how far away from home we happen to wander. When He finds us, He will lift us up into His arms for repair, rest, and nourishment—if we allow Him.

Father, when I am bruised and cut from
running down my own rebellious path,
too weak to even drag myself to You,
thank You for looking for me. And thank
You for picking me up and bringing me
home to safety. Amen

Surely you know.
Surely you have heard.
The LORD is the God who lives
forever, who created all the world.
He does not become tired or need to rest.

ISAIAH 40:28 NCV

A CAT IS A LION IN A
JUNGLE OF SMALL BUSHES.

INDIAN PROVERB

CIVILIZATION IS DEFINED
BY THE PRESENCE OF CATS.

ANONYMOUS

PROWLING HIS OWN QUIET
BACKYARD OR ASLEEP BY THE FIRE,
HE IS STILL ONLY A WHISKER
AWAY FROM THE WILDS.

JEAN BURDEN

No Backing Out

Twice in his life, Gato experienced the pain of kidney stones. One episode required catheterization for ten days, during which he had to wear a cone collar that prevented him from removing the catheter. We put him in the large central bathroom where he could be easily encouraged by family members.

Gato's immediate goal was to pull out the catheter. He spent hours maneuvering himself into positions he hoped would help him back out of his collar, but each attempt failed.

Although we visited him often, our distractions were only temporary, for he quickly returned to his obsession of trying to back out of the collar. With all efforts exhausted, he often sat down and hissed in frustration.

"Why don't you just relax, Gato?" I asked one day, sitting on the edge of the tub. "You make it much harder than it has to be. That collar will stay on for ten days. Nothing you do will make me remove it earlier. So why not make the best of it, sweetheart?"

God then reminded me that I, too, often attempt to wriggle out of an uncomfortable situation. Like Gato, I think my restriction is the problem. If I can just manage to work my way out of the tight spot, everything will be fine. Could it be that what appears to me to be a useless and frustrating period of time, one that seems to only prevent me from reaching my goal, may in reality be God's goal for me? A time for me to develop patience, strengthen trust, and allow healing of long-ignored wounds?

Maybe I should take my own advice: Just relax and wait for God's perfect timing.

Heavenly Father, when I am frustrated
during the dark stretches of life, help
me to recognize them as opportunities
for growth. And remind me that some
plants grow best in the dark. Amen

I will give you the treasures of darkness
And hidden riches of secret places.

ISAIAH 45:3 NKJV

THE MAN WHO CARRIES A CAT
BY THE TAIL LEARNS SOMETHING
THAT CAN BE LEARNED IN NO OTHER WAY.

MARK TWAIN

DOGS HAVE OWNERS,
CATS HAVE STAFF.

ANONYMOUS

THE CAT IS NATURE'S BEAUTY.

FRENCH PROVERB

No Help Needed

Some mornings I put Gato outside on the deck because I didn't want him underfoot, especially on those mornings when I had an early appointment. I preferred to prepare his breakfast without his assistance since he tried to second-guess my every move, often getting in my way and causing me to trip over him.

The doors and windows on the view side of our house contained glass that allowed those inside to see out but prevented those outside from seeing in. During the day it reflected as a mirror. On busy mornings I could see Gato, nose pressed to the pane, trying to determine what I was doing. His body expression clearly asked, "I wonder if she really is doing the things she should be doing to take care of my needs?"

I'd smile to myself and think, *Poor Gato, doesn't he know I would never forget to feed him?* (Well, almost never. I did once.) When his meal was ready, I'd open the door and let him in.

Sometimes I, too, feel frustrated because I can't see what God is doing on His side. It's like I've pressed my face against the windows of heaven and am trying to peer in. Has He forgotten about me? Is He really doing the things that are necessary to meet my needs? Does He even remember what they are? (Surely He does. All of heaven must know since I yowl so long and so loudly!)

Could it be that He does not allow me a glimpse of what He is doing because He knows I will get in the way? He knows how I try to second-guess His every action, how I offer suggestions as to how He can better do His job of meeting my needs, how I tend to give Him advice on how He should be handling my (and everyone else's) problems.

Like Gato, when I try to anticipate God's movements I often trip things up and hinder the progress. And I'm sure He recalls those times when I run off in a direction that I think He is going, but because I'm running in the wrong direction, I'm not in the right spot when He calls me. No wonder He doesn't let me know what He is doing!

And, unlike Gato's owner, God will never forget me. Not even once.

Heavenly Father, remind me that You will meet all of my needs when things are ready—and always in Your perfect time. Amen

Do not worry, saying, "What shall we eat?" or "What shall we drink?" or "What shall we wear?" . . . Your heavenly Father knows that you need all these things. But seek first the kingdom of God and His righteousness, and all these things shall be added to you.

MATTHEW 6:31-33 NKJV

CATS LOVE ONE SO MUCH—
MORE THAN THEY WILL ALLOW.
BUT THEY HAVE SO MUCH WISDOM
THEY KEEP IT TO THEMSELVES.

MARY WILKINS

IT IS A VERY INCONVENIENT
HABIT OF KITTENS THAT,
WHATEVER YOU SAY TO THEM,
THEY ALWAYS PURR.

LEWIS CARROLL

Purr, Purr

As verbal as Gato could be when he was hungry or wanted to be let in or out, I must admit that most of the time he demanded nothing from me. Sometimes, when I sat at my computer, he would appear by my desk and sit quietly until I noticed him. Although he demanded nothing, I knew what he wanted: to be near me.

When I patted my thigh he'd jump onto my lap for no reason other than to love and be loved. I'd take time to stroke him and whisper how much I loved him. He'd nuzzle my hand, lick it, lean against me, and then purr himself to sleep.

How often do I go to the Lord merely to let Him know that I love Him and to rest in His love? I usually barge into His presence with a long list of demands and whine persistently over every need.

Why don't I go to Him in love just because I want to be close to Him, to relax contentedly in His loving arms and enjoy being in His presence? I am certain it would be a pleasant experience for both of us.

Father, I love You. I want nothing at
this moment other than to lean against
You and enjoy Your love. Amen

There is a time for everything, and a
season for every activity under heaven . . .
a time to be silent . . . a time to love.

ECCLESIASTES 3:1, 7-8 NIV

FOR HE PURRS IN THANKFULNESS
WHEN GOD TELLS HIM HE IS A GOOD CAT.

CHRISTOPHER SMART

IF THERE WERE TO BE A UNIVERSAL
SOUND DEPICTING PEACE, I WOULD
SURELY VOTE FOR THE PURR.

BARBARA L. DIAMOND

WHEN I'M DISCOURAGED,
HE'S EMPATHY INCARNATE,
PURRING AND RUBBING TO
TELEGRAPH HIS DISMAY.

CATHERYN JAKOBSON

A CAT CAN PURR ITS
WAY OUT OF ANYTHING.

DONNA MCCROHAN

Rain, Rain, Go Away

It was an unusually wet winter that year for central and northern California. Only three days out of January did it not rain. Gato became very impatient. He wanted to roam outside, chase squirrels and gophers, and meander down to the creek. He didn't want to surf.

One evening he sat by the sliding glass door in the back of our house peering out into the darkness. I knew he was longing for what he hoped would be outside—a lovely moonlit night. As I passed him I commented, "Gato, you don't want to go out there. It's cold and the wind is blowing icy rain across the deck." He wanted out anyway and let me know.

I slowly opened the door, just enough for him to poke his head out. He squinted his eyes and braced himself against the wind, tail switching madly. Midway through the door opening, he stopped. As the cold rain hit him in the face, he brought his head back in and gave me a look that clearly said, "You've got to be kidding!"

"It was your idea," I said. As I closed the door, I noted his determined walk down the hall to the front door. "The weather is no different there," I called out.

Determined to find another avenue that would give him what he wanted, he sat by the front door and waited. "All right, but you'll see that the weather is the same regardless of which door you go through." I flipped on the porch light, opened the front door, and we both stepped out under the protection of the overhang.

I watched as he looked beyond the front porch out into the blackness. Nothing but driving rain. He peered around the corner of the house, following the wet deck with his eyes. Nothing but more rain. He sat down and contemplated the situation for a moment, then looked up into my face and hissed several times in frustration.

"I'm sorry," I said as I followed him in, "but I have no control over the weather."

I know how Gato feels. No matter what door I try to escape through to avoid life's stormy circumstances, I can't. I, too, often hiss in frustration at my heavenly Father.

"Can't you make the rain go away?" I'll pray. He is not disturbed by these outbursts, however, because He understands my longings.

When I've exhausted my fruitless efforts, He patiently and lovingly encourages me through the bad weather with His soothing words. His words comfort me because, unlike Gato's owner, God can control the weather. He'll either stop the rain or keep me safe inside His arms until the storm passes over.

Father, thank You for Your patience
when I am frustrated over life's
inclement circumstances. Thank You for
knowing my heart even better than I
do, and for standing beside me through
all the bad weather. Amen

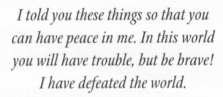

*I told you these things so that you
can have peace in me. In this world
you will have trouble, but be brave!
I have defeated the world.*

JOHN 16:33 NCV

MOST CATS WHEN THEY
ARE OUT WANT TO BE IN,
AND VICE VERSA, AND
OFTEN SIMULTANEOUSLY.
LOUIS J. CAMUTI, D.V.M.

THE MATHEMATICAL PROBABILITY
OF A COMMON CAT DOING
EXACTLY AS IT PLEASES IS THE ONE
SCIENTIFIC ABSOLUTE IN THE WORLD.
LYNN M. OSBAND

A CAT POURS HIS BODY
ON THE FLOOR LIKE WATER.
IT IS RESTFUL JUST TO SEE HIM.
WILLIAM LYON PHELPS

Impressions

Gato liked to sleep at the foot of our bed on a large down-filled comforter, handmade for us by Tamara. Each morning when I made the bed, I'd fluff out the area where he slept and contemplate how the full weight of his body during the night leaves an impression that remains long after he is gone, visible evidence of where he has rested.

I wish I could rest in my heavenly Father so completely that I could let the full weight of my being lean on Him during the dark hours. What a joy it would be to relax in the comfort of His care so completely that there would be visible evidence that I had done so! Not so I can impress those around me, but so they can see the impression my Comforter makes upon me.

Father, help me to trust and rest in You so that others may be comforted when they see You in me. Amen

Praise be to the God and Father of our
Lord Jesus Christ. God is the Father
who is full of mercy and all comfort.
He comforts us every time we have trouble,
so when others have trouble, we can comfort
them with the same comfort God gives us.

2 CORINTHIANS 1:3, 4 NCV

CATS DO CARE.
FOR EXAMPLE THEY KNOW
INSTINCTIVELY WHAT TIME WE
HAVE TO BE AT WORK IN THE
MORNING AND THEY WAKE US
UP TWENTY MINUTES BEFORE
THE ALARM GOES OFF.

MICHAEL NELSON

I CARE NOT MUCH FOR A MAN'S
RELIGION WHOSE DOG AND CAT
ARE NOT THE BETTER FOR IT.

ABRAHAM LINCOLN

CATS CAN WORK OUT
MATHEMATICALLY THE EXACT
PLACE TO SIT THAT WILL CAUSE
MOST INCONVENIENCE.

PAM BROWN

Beating Up What?

In the dimly lit hall one night, I saw a strange-looking black bug on the floor. Grabbing my shoe, I shuddered as I beat it again and again. Was it a scorpion, a summer roach that had crept in from outside, or a black widow that had intruded our domain? *Whatever it was, it certainly will never move again,* I thought triumphantly. I shoved it to the side of the wall with my shoe and returned to bed.

Entering the hall the next morning, I recalled the incident and bent down to inspect the remains of my beating episode the night before. In the light of day, I could clearly see what it was—a patch of Gato's black fur.

As I picked it up, I exclaimed out loud, "This is the cause of all of my fear and retaliation?" I felt foolish and looked around for someone to blame.

I saw Gato sitting by his empty food bowl. Gato! Had he not shed his fur all over the house, this wouldn't have happened.

The truth is, had I turned the light on I would have seen clearly what it was. And had I not been remiss in Gato's daily brushings, there would have been no loose fur to shed.

So like me! Sometimes when I am in the dark as to the facts regarding an individual or circumstance, I flail away—fighting I know not what to protect myself from an assumed threat. Why do I misjudge others and then look around for someone else to blame for my own foolish actions, when all I have to do is just turn on the light?

Lord, help me to walk in Your light so that I may not stumble in the areas of good judgment. Amen

If we say we have fellowship with God,
but we continue living in darkness,
we are liars and do not follow the truth.
But if we live in the light, as God is in the light,
we can share fellowship with each other.
Then the blood of Jesus, God's Son,
cleanses us from every sin.

1 JOHN 1:6-7 NCV

IF MAN COULD BE CROSSED WITH
THE CAT IT WOULD IMPROVE MAN,
BUT IT WOULD DETERIORATE THE CAT.

MARK TWAIN

ESSENTIALLY, YOU DO NOT SO MUCH
TEACH YOUR CAT AS BRIBE HIM.

LYNN HOLLYN

NO TAME ANIMAL HAS LOST LESS OF
ITS NATIVE DIGNITY OR MAINTAINED
MORE OF ITS ANCIENT RESERVE.
THE DOMESTIC CAT MIGHT REBEL TOMORROW.

WILLIAM CONWAY

THE CAT IS THE ANIMAL TO WHOM
THE CREATOR GAVE THE BIGGEST EYE,
THE SOFTEST FUR, THE MOST SUPREMELY
DELICATE NOSTRILS, A MOBILE EAR,
AN UNRIVALED PAW, AND A CURVED CLAW
BORROWED FROM THE ROSE-TREE.

COLETTE

Rough Waters

"Want to go for a walk?" I called out, disrupting Gato's nap. He jumped up and headed toward the door. He loved to go for walks, especially to the creek.

Although the earth was soggy and the grass was wet, Gato enjoyed his walk—that is, until we got to the edge of the rocky pathway that revealed the roaring waters below. The rainy winter had filled our creek and waterfall with icy water, spilling from the hills and mountains high above the valley.

I dashed down the path and stood at the edge of the waterfall, in awe of its power and force. Gato observed me from the top of a large rock. When I called for him to come down and join me, he gave me a look that said, "Not on your life!"

I stood for a few minutes taking in the beauty—the lacy ferns, the velvet green of the moss-covered rocks, and the misty rain falling gently through the air. Across the valley and beyond the mountains, the sun glowed through patchy clouds.

As I turned, I saw Gato jump onto the path and bound toward me. I picked him up and gently stroked him. I felt his body tremble and press closer to me as he stared into the tumbling waters below.

When facing the raging waters of life, I wish I could respond as quickly in trust to my heavenly Father. When He calls me to walk with Him I prefer to pick and choose the paths we take. I'll pass on the floods, the dark skies, and the mighty winds, thank you. I am definitely a fair-weather child! Call me when the waters die down, the sun comes out, and the birds resume singing.

Yet my sweetest memories are those of pressing close to my Savior, secure in His strong arms during overwhelming difficulties. Because I followed His call, albeit slowly, I emerged with a stronger trust in Him, and with less fear of life's raging waters.

Father, when You call, remind me that Your love is awesome in its power! It is greater than the mighty forces of nature, greater than any circumstance, and greater than all of the evils of darkness. Help me to look up and see the light of Your Son through the patchy clouds. Amen

Fear not for I have redeemed you;
I have summoned you by name; you are mine.
When you pass through the waters,
I will be with you . . . they will not sweep over you
. . . for I am the LORD your God . . . your Savior . . .
since you are precious and honored
in my sight, and because I love you.

ISAIAH 43:1-4 NIV

How you behave toward cats here below
determines your status in Heaven.
ROBERT A. HEINLEIN

There is nothing sweeter than his peace
when at rest, for there is nothing
brisker than his life when in motion.
CHRISTOPHER SMART

A cat can be trusted to purr
when she is pleased,
which is more than can be said
for human beings.
WILLIAM INGE

Exit or Entrance?

It was hard for Gato to leave his mountain home paradise and move to an apartment in the desert. No longer could he watch the deer graze beyond the fence from our deck, walk with me down to the creek, and sit with me as we listened to the music of the waterfall in the spring. And he missed the antics of the baby squirrels as they ran up and down the huge oak tree by our breakfast nook window.

Gato disliked his new surroundings—the tiny apartment, the strange smells, and, most of all, his new harness and leash. On our nightly walks, he often sat down and balked, hissing in frustration.

Jerry and I understood. After years of living with cats, we're fluent in Hiss. But Gato was going to have to adjust. We all missed the mountain home. We had designed that home, our dream home, inch by inch. We had pushed through thick brush and trees to lay out its boundaries. Each window on the west side focused on the breathtaking view of the Oakhurst Valley nestled in the foothills of the Sierra Nevadas near Yosemite National Park. Our living room window was centered on Deadwood Mountain, a majestic sight in the winter, with its glistening coat of white armor as it guarded the valley between us. To its right, Windy Gap provided the perfect view for the glorious sunsets of summer evenings. I had single-handedly dug and rock-trimmed seventeen beds for the roses that rewarded us so generously with their fragrant beauty. It had been our plan to live there forever. The last thing on earth we wanted to do was leave.

But circumstances change and lives are affected. As the California economy sagged, our successful business slowly slipped downhill. Despite the use of all of our retirement funds, we could not salvage it. We ultimately said goodbye to our faithful employees and closed the company's doors forever.

Then God led us to an area in which I said I would never live—the desert. But Arizona was where God wanted us. It provided a booming economy with bountiful job opportunities, the perfect place to start all over again.

It was difficult to step over the ashes of our business and leave our mountain home to the care of tenants. Nearing retirement age, the hardest step for us was submitting to a new economic harness and leash by working for strangers in a new land.

Like Gato, we, too, often hissed in frustration, but we knew we were not alone. The presence of our heavenly Father assured us that He understood as He gently tugged at us each step of the way. Despite our questionings, He had everything under control.

Heavenly Father, help us to be as faithful in following You as You are in leading us. Thank You for the assurance that You want what is best for us. May we give our best to You in every new land. Amen

"For I know the plans I have for you," declares the LORD, *"plans to prosper you and not to harm you, plans to give you hope and a future."*

JEREMIAH 29:11 NIV

OUR WORDS SHOULD BE PURRS INSTEAD OF HISSES.

KATHRINE PALMER PETERSON

IT IS IN THE NATURE OF CATS TO DO
A CERTAIN AMOUNT OF UNESCORTED ROAMING.

ADLAI STEVENSON

OF ALL GOD'S CREATURES, THERE IS ONLY ONE
THAT CANNOT BE MADE SLAVE OF THE LEASH.
THAT ONE IS THE CAT.

MARK TWAIN

NO MATTER HOW HARD YOU TRY TO TEACH YOUR CAT
GENERAL RELATIVITY, YOU'RE GOING TO FAIL.

BRIAN GREENE

WHEN YOU COME UPON YOUR CAT DEEP
IN MEDITATION, STARING THOUGHTFULLY
AT SOMETHING THAT YOU CAN'T SEE,
JUST REMEMBER THAT YOUR CAT IS,
IN FACT, RUNNING THE UNIVERSE.

BONNI ELIZABETH HALL

Entrance

Gato ran at full speed through each room of our new house. "You really love your new home, don't you, Gato?" I called out to him as he streaked past me into the great room. He made a quick U-turn and zoomed toward me, stopping at my feet to grin up at me. He had not done that since we moved from California. Now it was a daily routine. He was ecstatic to finally be free of the confines of the apartment. He had his own pet door, his own private backyard, and in the far corner a 600-pound sandbox built by Jerry that resembled a golf bunker. No more harness and leash. He could run and do as he pleased!

One day, two years after our move into that house, Gato sat purring in my lap. We were both resting from playing his favorite game of "Let me chase you through the house and you squeal when I catch you and I whack you on the leg with my paw." I stroked him lovingly and said, "God certainly knew what He was doing when he brought us to Arizona, didn't He, Gato?" He looked up and responded with a half meow, muffled by a yawn. "I'll never forget how happy you were to be free of your harness and leash when we moved out of the apartment. Well, now I'm free of mine. I just took early retirement. That's why we have more time to chase each other through the house and play hide-and-seek."

I leaned back and reflected. How Jerry and I had struggled under God's harness and leash as He led us from our California mountain home to Arizona. During the ensuing years, it continued to be difficult as Jerry and I went to work daily in separate directions on different shifts, rarely seeing each other. There was little time for Gato. He often looked at me as I rushed out the door as if to say, I think you've forgotten me. And I would call over my shoulder, "I haven't forgotten you, sweetheart. Someday we will have more time together. I promise."

Well, someday was finally here.

There were times when Jerry and I thought God had forgotten us and His promise to us. But He hadn't. He had opened a new door, one with much more opportunity than the door that had slammed shut in California. With God's leadership, Jerry and a capable partner, Tom, had started their own business, one that was growing beyond all expectations, one that allowed me to quit work and pursue my dreams.

Tears of gratitude dropped onto Gato's fur. When he looked up, I explained, "I'm not sad this time, Gato. I am rejoicing because of God's love and faithfulness. We are now realizing the fruits of His promise."

As Gato resumed his contented doze in my lap, I whispered a prayer of thanks.

Thank You, Lord, for leading us to this new land. Thank You for ignoring all of our balkings, hissings, and strainings at the leash because we could not see Your plan for us. Amen

LORD, you have made me happy by
what you have done; I will sing for joy
about what your hands have done.
LORD, you have done such great things!
How deep are your thoughts!

PSALM 92:4-5 NCV

WHO WOULD BELIEVE SUCH
PLEASURE FROM A WEE BALL O' FUR?

IRISH SAYING

A MEOW MASSAGES THE HEART.

STUART MCMILLAN

THERE ARE FEW THINGS IN LIFE
MORE HEART WARMING THAN
TO BE WELCOMED BY A CAT.

TAY HOHOFF

Goodbye to a Friend

"I want to take him home and spend these last few hours with him," I whispered through trembling lips. Why was I speaking so softly? Gato wouldn't understand the significance of my words. But maybe if I spoke quietly, the pounding of my heart would slow a little.

It had happened so quickly. Only two weeks earlier, I had taken Gato to the vet for what I thought was a routine exam. His earliest symptoms were weakening hind legs that sometimes wobbled. A touch of arthritis, we thought. However, his lethargy and diminished appetite had prompted a visit to the vet.

After careful examination, lab tests, and x-rays, Dr. Watson went over the information with me. She explained that Gato had kidney problems and would need medication for the rest of his life. It was bad news, but nothing had appeared life-threatening at that visit. In fact, in the following weeks, he appeared to be improving. Then Gato suddenly developed labored breathing (we learned later that he had cancer of the pancreas, kidney, and lungs), and here we were again at the vet this fateful Monday morning.

Following an extensive examination and review of all reports and x-rays, the doctor said the words all pet lovers fear: "We need to put him down. He is in great discomfort. I doubt if he will last through the night."

I called my husband at the office and he came home. Together, we spent that last special afternoon with our cherished feline friend.

"I want to be with Gato when he is given his injection," I said firmly, afraid that Jerry might object. "I do not want him to go alone."

"Me too," he said. "Besides, he has always been his happiest when the three of us are together."

In the examining room that evening, the vet softly explained that Gato would suffer no pain from the injection. His only discomfort would be the insertion of the needle, which contained a sedative overdose. After sixty seconds, he would simply go to sleep. Then she left us alone to be with Gato.

Encircled by my arms, Gato purred weakly as he lay on the table. Jerry and I caressed him and stroked his ears with love words. My tears wet his fur a final time as I whispered, "Thank you, dear Gato, for the love and joy you have brought into our home these wonderful fifteen years."

The time came and the injection was given. "Goodbye, dear friend," we whispered sadly. Still encircled in my arms, Gato received my last kiss as he laid his head in Jerry's hands and went to sleep.

Thank you, Lord, for the gift of pets that enrich our lives so dearly. Though their years are short, their memories live on. And we are better and wiser for having known them. Amen

"Ask the animals, and they will teach you."

JOB 12:7 NCV

GOD ALLOWS CATS INTO HEAVEN
JUST SO HE CAN KEEP AN EYE ON THEM.
DIXIE CARTER

SINCE EACH OF US IS BLESSED WITH ONLY
ONE LIFE, WHY NOT LIVE IT WITH A CAT?
ROBERT STEARNS

IF CLEANLINESS IS NEXT TO GODLINESS,
SURELY OUR CATS MUST GO TO HEAVEN
AND SIT ON THE ARM OF GOD'S THRONE.
JERRY CLIMER

A Place for Miss Middy

"Genie, our special feature guest, needs to find a home for her cat—a black and white longhaired Norwegian beauty," announced the chairman during our Christian Women's Club luncheon. A board member smiled and pointed to me. I slid further down into my chair and waved her off in protest. But Genie saw me.

Since the demise of El Gato Gordo, it seemed as though the whole world was trying to foist some needy cat upon us. But Jerry and I had agreed that we needed a rest. Although we'd loved our cats, they were a big responsibility. Besides, Jerry planned to retire soon and we had extensive travel plans.

After the luncheon I bolted for the door, but Genie intercepted me and pitched her plea. "We love Miss Middy, but we can't keep her." Genie then recounted their extensive but fruitless efforts to place Miss Middy. Noting my resistance she resorted to begging. "Please, just pray about it. I know God has the perfect place for Miss Middy, but we're running out of time. We need to find a home for her this week or we'll have to put her to sleep," she pled, lips quivering. A tear trickled down her face.

She's not playing fair! I thought resentfully. *Now I'm supposed to feel guilty if I don't take this cat—which will die if I don't. That's hitting below the belt!*

I hadn't the slightest interest in her cat. Yet, strangely, at the peak of my resistance, I found myself fighting a subtle awareness that our home was meant to be Miss Middy's destination. I wasn't about to budge, but I did promise Genie I'd pray about the matter and give her my answer in a few days.

I'm not taking this cat! I thought defiantly as I drove home. *I don't know why I even promised to pray about it. It's just wasting valuable time—time Genie could use to look elsewhere for a suitable home.*

By the time I drove into my driveway, however, I was overwhelmed by the feeling that ours was to be Miss Middy's home. But still I resisted, and went straight to the Top:

"God, I can't believe You don't have more important things to do than to be concerned about finding a home for this cat. And for some strange reason, I think You want her for Jerry—which doesn't make sense. He's made it clear that we are to have no more cats until we are retired and through with our traveling. Besides, he has said countless times that when we do get another cat, he wants a kitten. One that will have lots of energy to jump and play, not just lie around. Miss Middy is no kitten—she is almost five years old!"

I waited but there was no heavenly response.

Jerry was out of state attending a glass convention. I still had two days before he got back, so there was no rush to make a decision. But who can win an argument with God? A few hours later I called with my decision, and a relieved but tearful Genie delivered Miss Middy to our home the next day.

That night when Jerry called, I took steps to prepare him.

"Since you're coming home on St. Patrick's Day, I have a present for you," I announced—a little too brightly.

"Since when do we exchange gifts on St. Patrick's Day?" he asked.

"We don't. And you don't need to get me anything. This is just a s-purr-of-the-moment gift I picked up for you. Well, actually, I didn't pick it up—it was delivered, but—oh, you'll understand later."

After Jerry's return home, we were chatting in the living room when his gift sauntered in and sat down. She fixed large pale green eyes on Jerry, quietly assessing him, until he turned and saw her.

"What is this?" he asked in a falsetto voice, openly impressed by her beauty.

"This is Miss Middy, your St. Patrick's Day gift," I bubbled. Jerry accepted her graciously but with less enthusiasm. I flinched at the disappointment in his eyes as he watched our cat-free traveling plans fly out the window.

I tried to explain how I hadn't really wanted the cat but for some strange reason I'd felt a strong nudging from God to accept her. For Jerry. But I didn't know why. His expression clearly said, "Yeah, right. You really got her for yourself, using me as the scapegoat and blaming it all on God. After all, who can argue when a person says, 'God told me to do this' and then hands you a gift you don't want?"

Miss Middy quickly adjusted to the peace and quiet of our home. Before long, she became "Daddy's girl"—a miracle in itself since Genie had warned me that Miss Middy didn't care for men.

It was too soon for either of us to see any logic in God's plan. Though we grew to love Miss Middy, we suspected that God's intervention had been more in her best interest than ours. But as always, God had bigger plans.

Six months later, Jerry was diagnosed with cancer. He needed immediate treatment for non-Hodgkin's lymphoma. Weakened and uncomfortable from his resulting radiation treatments, Jerry looked forward to his times of relaxation with Miss Middy, who had become his constant companion. Often I walked into the room at night to find him in his reclining chair with Miss Middy draped across the top of the headrest, one paw lying gently on top of his head, the other on his shoulder—both sound asleep.

Genie's prayers were, indeed, answered. God found the perfect place for Miss Middy—in Jerry's hurting heart.

Thank you, Lord, for meeting our needs
even before they are apparent. Amen

Your Father knows what you need before you ask Him.

MATTHEW 6:8 NIV

ONE CAT JUST LEADS TO ANOTHER.

ERNEST HEMINGWAY (WHO HAD 30 CATS)

THERE ARE TWO MEANS OF
REFUGE FROM THE MISERIES
OF LIFE: MUSIC AND CATS.

ALBERT SCHWEITZER

CATS ARE LOVE ON FOUR LEGS.

RICHARD TORREGROSSA

Miss Middy's Adversary

Several months after Miss Middy came to live with us, we moved into a lakefront home. We worried about yet another adjustment for Middy, but she immediately fell in love with her new backyard. She often sat among the foxtail ferns and flowers beneath the huge mesquite tree and gazed out over the manmade lake. She watched with interest as mallards swam lazily in the cove. Sometimes she chased lizards as they scampered from rock to rock. But mostly, she just dozed.

One morning as she napped peacefully in her Garden of Eden, a loud shriek pierced the early morning stillness. Middy bolted awake as a flying object hit her from the rear. Again and again it attacked from different directions. Middy hunkered down and tried to creep in retreat to the patio sliding door with some dignity, but sharp beak attacks prevented her advance. The silky fur on her back and tail was pulled at viciously. Miss Middy's paradise was under siege—by a mama mockingbird. A partially hidden nest of baby birds could be seen directly overhead in the tree branches.

For several days, I observed this recurring drama with interest from the bay window. *She's bigger than that bird,* I thought. *Why doesn't she just turn and fight her attacker?* But each day Miss Middy crawled inch by inch in humiliating retreat toward the safety of our patio door where I stood ready to let her in.

One morning, however, the routine changed. As I again observed Middy's embarrassing retreat by belly, she stopped. Springing suddenly to her full height, she turned and faced her tormentor. With bared fangs and a loud hiss, she swatted at the bird, narrowly missing it. The bird quickly flew away.

It was apparent that as long as Miss Middy retreated in fear, she definitely was losing the battle. But once she turned and courageously faced her adversary, the attacker fled.

One would think Miss Middy might learn from this experience. And yet each spring day this drama repeated itself until the baby birds were strong enough to fly away—without ever being bothered by Middy. Though the mockingbird ignored Middy after that, I knew it would be back during the next nesting season.

Will Miss Middy be any wiser when that time comes? I wondered.

Reminds me of my battles. I fear that I, too, am a slow learner. Once I tire of crawling in defeat and instead turn and face my Adversary, he leaves. But I know he will be back. I hope I have learned something in his absence.

Help me to remember, Lord, that because of who I am in You, I am bigger than any problem. With Your help I can face and overcome any situation. Amen

---

You are of God, little children,
and have overcome them, because
He who is in you is greater than
he who is in the world.

1 JOHN 4:4 NKJV

Resist the devil and he will flee from you.

JAMES 4:7 NKJV

A CAT PENT UP BECOMES A LION.

CAT PROVERB

THERE IS, INDEED,
NO SINGLE QUALITY OF THE
CAT THAT MAN COULD NOT
EMULATE TO HIS ADVANTAGE.

CARL VAN VECHTEN

WE HUMANS ARE INDEED
FORTUNATE IF WE HAPPEN TO BE
CHOSEN TO BE OWNED BY A CAT.

ANONYMOUS

In Position

"Why is Miss Middy sitting at the foot of the stairs yowling?" Jerry asked as he walked into the kitchen.

Placing the last of the lunch dishes into the dishwasher, I replied, "Because she wants a nap."

"You've got to be kidding! Since when does she ask if she can take a nap? That's all she does," he commented with a grin.

"Well, this time she wants me to take a nap with her."

"Oh, yeah, right. And how do you know that?"

"It started last week. Remember that night I was on a roll with my writing and stayed up until 3:00 in the morning? I thought I could make it all day without a nap but I couldn't. After lunch I decided I'd take a power nap and set my timer for fifteen minutes—I learned that from a doctor I worked for years ago. It's amazing how refreshed you can feel in such a short time. If you sleep longer than fifteen minutes, everything slows down and you feel worse when you get up," I explained, getting sidetracked.

"What does that have to do with Middy?"

"She happened to be watching when I lay down on our bed, so she jumped up and took a nap with me. She evidently thought that was special. Every day since then, she wants me to go take a nap—in our bed—with her."

"And you do it?"

"Not always. But she's so cute, I can't resist sometimes. After yowling, she catches my eye to make sure I'm watching, and then she runs to the top of the stairs and stops. When she's sure I'm following, she runs into the bedroom and jumps on the bed. I don't always have the need or the time for a power nap, but I often go up and just snuggle with her a few minutes until she drifts to sleep—like I used to do with our babies—and then I slip out of the room."

"That is one spoiled kitty!" Jerry said affectionately as he poured himself a fresh glass of iced tea.

I finished up in the kitchen and reflected on Miss Middy's skill at communicating her needs. It's not that she just asks; she also gets into position. When she wants outside, she sits by the door. When she wants Jerry to snuggle with her, she sits by his recliner. When she wants to be brushed, she sits on the brushing rug. When she needs food or water, she sits next to her empty bowls. When she craves her favorite snack, she sits on the floor beneath the vitamin drawer. When she wants to do serious napping without me, she goes to the bedroom closet and calls. I open the door and she jumps up on the purse shelf, the half that I've left clear for her, and she naps. Middy learned the effectiveness of getting into position to have her needs met soon after she arrived at our house.

I wish I could have learned that lesson as quickly.

I recall a difficult period in my life when I stopped going to church. I lost focus of my Creator when I became disillusioned with some of His creations. "They're all hypocrites!" I decided. "I'm a Christian—I don't have to go to church for God to love me." So I stopped going.

Soon, staying away from God's house became a habit. But instead of feeling better, I felt worse—alone and empty deep inside. It seemed like my prayers never went higher than the ceiling. I begged God to meet the needs of my life and my heart, but how could He? I was not in position. Once I returned to church and called out to Him with all my needs, He never failed to meet them. I must admit, however, that amid all the love and blessings heaped upon me during the many years since returning to His house, I often feel like one spoiled Kitty!

Dear Lord, May I never again leave Your house because I am distracted by circumstances or people. May I always know the joy of Your personal attention by being in the right position all the time—in the center of Your will. Amen

I was glad when they said to me,
"Let us go into the house of the LORD."

PSALM 122:1 NKJV

Surely goodness and mercy shall
follow me all the days of my life;
And I will dwell in the house
of the LORD forever.

PSALM 23:6 NKJV

THE CAT HAS NINE LIVES:

THREE FOR PLAYING,

THREE FOR STRAYING,

THREE FOR STAYING.

ENGLISH PROVERB

ONCE CATS WERE ALL WILD,

BUT AFTERWARD THEY RETIRED TO HOUSES.

EDWARD TOPSELL

DOGS COME WHEN THEY ARE CALLED;

CATS TAKE A MESSAGE AND GET BACK TO YOU.

MARY BLY

Nothing Ventured, Nothing Gained

As Miss Middy sat near the edge of the dock watching me feed the huge catfish our leftover table scraps, a friend from down the lake came by in her boat. She pulled up to chat for a minute. Middy fixed huge, fascinated eyes upon my friend's two Abyssinians, sitting aloof on the table in the boat, perfectly relaxed. They peered down at landlocked Middy, who stared at them in amazement. Maybe it was my imagination, but I thought I saw a glimmer of admiration in Middy's eyes and a hint of pity in theirs as the boat sped away.

The Abyssinians didn't know it, but their owner had just shared with me how terrified her show cats had been on their first boat ride. But after a few trips they became seasoned sailors and loved it.

As we walked up the steps to our patio I asked Middy, "Wouldn't you like to go out on the boat sometimes? That looks like fun, huh?" I'm not sure she understood my question even though her response sounded an awful lot like "Naoo!" I, however, thought it was a good idea.

"Middy needs to have her horizons expanded," I said later to Jerry, who instantly agreed. So it was two against one. We decided to take Middy out the next evening for a boat ride. This definitely was not a good idea as far as Middy was concerned. I scooped her up from the patio while Jerry readied the pontoon boat. She wasn't too worried until she realized she was going with me into the boat. She froze with fear, then struggled with every ounce of her twelve pounds, but I held her tightly. I didn't release her until we were far enough away from the dock that she wouldn't try to jump ship and swim to shore.

At first she huddled close to my feet and wouldn't budge. She made little gagging sounds, like she would heave. "That's okay, honey, you're just nervous and afraid, you'll get over it." She soon relaxed a little and rubbed against my leg. Jerry called to her in soothing tones from his captain's chair. "Miss Middy, come and see me. You can sit in my lap where there's a better view." But she wouldn't move.

I, however, moved to the backseat where I could sit close to Jerry and hold his hand. We ignored Middy and enjoyed the beautiful moonlit night and our soft jazz music. Midway through the ride, Middy began to relax and investigate the boat, but she still wasn't sold on the idea of traveling on water.

Yes, the first few trips were nerve-wracking for Middy, but before long she thoroughly enjoyed our boat rides. She loved to sit high on the table so everyone on shore or in passing boats could admire her beauty. She often stood on her hind legs for long periods of time with front paws dangling, like a standing squirrel, just watching the scenery go by. Every so often, dogs would run out and go crazy when they saw Middy, who never flinched—she just gave them a look of disdain. She'd turn and catch our eyes as if to say, "What can you expect from such noisy creatures? They're dogs."

Though she was terrified in the beginning, Miss Middy soon was very much at home on the water. Once she overcame her fear, she became adventuresome. Having sat everywhere on the boat, she once yowled loudly in frustration because she could not find a way to climb up on top of the canopy—and we refused to let her try.

"Well, guess that's proof our little Miss Middy has conquered her fear," Jerry announced proudly.

I remember the time I had to face my greatest fear. My stomach tied up in knots, and I feared I would heave. I couldn't move. There was no escape and no turning back and swimming for the shore. I was committed. So, after my introduction, I walked with wobbly knees to the podium and grasped the microphone.

We are told by experts that of the ten greatest fears people have, the number one fear is speaking in front of groups—just above the fear of snakes. For a long time God had nudged me to speak. I suggested He send someone else. He reminded me I was the only one who could do it—it was my story He wanted me to tell. But I was so afraid!

That was twenty-five years ago. What once sent icy slivers of fear into my heart now brings warm currents of joy to the deepest part of my soul. All because I ventured into the scary waters of public speaking.

Dear God, May I never be afraid when You call Me to do anything that takes Me out of My comfort zone. Remind Me that you are the Great Comforter and will equip Me to do whatever you ask. Otherwise, You would have never called Me. Amen

Fear not, for I am with you;
Be not dismayed, for I am your God.
I will strengthen you, Yes, I will help you,
I will uphold you with My righteous right hand.

ISAIAH 41:10 NKJV

THE CAT LOVES FISH BUT DOES
NOT WISH TO WET ITS FEET.

CAT PROVERB

BECAUSE OF OUR WILLINGNESS TO
ACCEPT CATS AS SUPERHUMAN
CREATURES, THEY ARE THE IDEAL ANIMALS
WITH WHICH TO WORK CREATIVELY.

RONI SCHOTTER

A CAT WILL NEVER DROWN
IF SHE SEES THE SHORE.

FRANCIS BACON

'Father, May I?'

Draining water from the steaming pasta into the sink, I was vaguely aware of Miss Middy's meow. Then I heard Jerry's query from the family room, "What does Middy want?"

"I don't know. Why don't you ask her?" I countered with a grin.

Miss Middy was the most articulate of all our cats. She had a different verbalization for her every need.

"I did, but I still don't know what she wants. You try—you two seem to have a language all your own."

He was right. I usually knew exactly what Miss Middy wanted. I turned toward the sound of her voice and saw her sitting in the tiled pathway between the kitchen and the family room, staring at me.

"What do you want, Middy?" I asked, giving the spaghetti sauce a final stir. She told me, but I couldn't understand what she wanted either.

None of her feline words indicated a desire to go outside, snuggle, play a game, find her toy, take a nap, or watch for someone about to ring the doorbell. Nor did her meows indicate a complaint that her food or water bowl was empty or that her litter box needed attention. She just sat there and meowed, her big green eyes fixed on mine.

"I don't know what you want, sweetheart. Show me." She turned and walked straight through the kitchen, through the door into the dining area, with tail high in the air—her command for "Follow me," which I did obediently. She stopped at the table and sat down by the nearest dining room chair and again stared into my eyes.

I looked at her and with a shrug asked, "What?"

Middy meowed and looked up at the chair.

Maybe there's something in the chair, I thought, peering cautiously under the table at the white brocade chair cushion. I half expected to find a big dead bug or, worse, a live one. But nothing was there.

Our eyes met again, and she repeated her request a little slower, as if I hadn't understood the first time—which I hadn't.

"Middy, I don't have a clue. What do you want?"

Again, she looked up toward the chair. Suddenly, it hit me. *She's asking my permission to sit in this chair!*

Several weeks earlier, I had discovered her napping in that very chair. She was scolded soundly and told to "get down," which she did reluctantly.

Now, she is asking my permission? I couldn't believe it.

"Miss Middy," I said, "you know that is a no-no, you do not sit in that chair. Ever! That is definitely no!" I emphasized the *no* word, adding "And don't ask me again."

She looked longingly at the chair seat for a brief moment, then again locked her pleading eyes onto mine. "The subject is closed," I said, deliberately but softly. She hesitated, then slowly exited the room with the dignity of a queen who had just dismissed her audience.

How could Middy know the reasoning behind my refusal? To her it was the perfect place to sit where a slice of the late afternoon sun filtering through the window would bathe her in warmth as she dozed peacefully.

I knew, however, that saying no to her meant less vacuuming for me. It also avoided the possibility of our guests leaving with white cat hairs on their dark clothing—maybe never to return. Though Miss Middy hadn't the capacity to understand my refusal, she accepted my final answer and never asked again.

What a contrast between Middy and me! How many times do I go back and keep begging God to let me have my way about something when it is clear He has other plans for me! Yet I yowl repeatedly, as if He didn't hear me the first time. Hoping He will be persuaded by my persistence, I daily present my verbal list of suggestions as to how He might accomplish my desire. Why don't I just accept His answer graciously and walk away with the dignity that comes with being a daughter of the King?

Lord, give me grace to accept Your final answer when it is no. Help me to trust You and realize that You always have good reasons behind Your response— reasons that affect not only me, but others. Amen

O My Father, if it is possible,
let this cup pass from Me; nevertheless,
not as I will, but as You will.

MATTHEW 26:39 NKJV

CATS SEEM TO GO ON THE PRINCIPLE
THAT IT NEVER DOES ANY HARM
TO ASK FOR WHAT YOU WANT.

JOSEPH WOOD KRUTCH

A CAT SEES NO GOOD REASON
WHY IT SHOULD OBEY ANOTHER ANIMAL,
EVEN IF IT DOES STAND ON TWO LEGS.

SARAH THOMPSON

I SUSPECT THAT MANY AN AILUROPHOBE
(A PERSON WHO FEARS OR HATES CATS)
HATES CATS ONLY BECAUSE HE FEELS THEY
ARE BETTER PEOPLE THAN HE IS—MORE HONEST,
MORE SECURE, MORE LOVED, MORE WHATEVER HE IS NOT.

WINIFRED CARRIERE

Messing Up

Like all of the family cats before her (well, except for wild-spirited Single), Miss Middy quickly learned the house rules and adapted to them easily. But on very rare occasions she would break the most important rule of our house: never do any serious business anyplace other than in the litter box, which was always fresh and clean. (Well, almost always.)

On those rare times when, for no apparent reason to anyone, she ignored her litter box, I often heard her mournful cry as she entered the room. This was a special cry, one that I soon learned was an announcement of guilt. Then she would go hide behind a chair, with head bent low. And wait. Had she not sought me out and readily confessed, I would not have known of her misdeed until I discovered it. (I was grateful for that!)

Upon investigation, I quickly found the area of her error. Sensing the need for discipline before cleaning, I grabbed the squirt bottle of vinegar-flavored water and walked toward her. My heart ached when I saw her stiffen in anticipation. Gathering her tense body into my arms, she hid her face by pressing her head hard against my arm as I carried her to the scene of the crime. Placing her on the floor beside the evidence, I pointed out her infraction, and in a soft but firm voice, scolded her—"You know that is NO, Miss Middy. That is very bad!"

It broke my heart as I held her squirming body tightly and squirted her face lightly with her punishment. Never did I love her more than at the time I disciplined her. Nevertheless, I tossed her outside and watched as she methodically licked her "wounds." I knew it would be a long time before she made that mistake again. But it would happen.

Through tears, I thought, *Why do you do that, sweetheart, when you know it brings pain to both of us? And I know you don't want to do it.* But I knew the answer. She didn't know why.

Just like I don't know why I displease my heavenly Father—time and again. It's not something I really want to do. So why do I do it? How tiring it must be for Him to clean up after me when I am disobedient. What a mess I make when I react in anger and soil relationships.

But my heart quickens when I realize an important truth: If I can feel such love for a little animal when it breaks the rules, yet forgive it and pick it up again in greater love, how much more does my heavenly Father still love me in my disobedience? And because I hurt when Miss Middy hurts, I know God's heart must ache when He watches me suffer the consequences of my actions.

I just wish I could be more like Miss Middy and go to Him quickly with my confession. Then maybe I wouldn't quietly carry my guilt to a dark place and try to hide from Him for so long.

Thank you, Lord, for always picking me up in love and forgiving me when I mess up—even when You know I'll do it again. Amen

I do not understand the things I do.
I do not do what I want to do, and
I do the things I hate. . . . I want to do the
things that are good, but I do not do them.

ROMANS 7:15, 18 NCV

If we confess our sins, he will forgive our sins,
because we can trust God to do what is right.
He will cleanse us from all the wrongs we have done.

1 JOHN 1:9 NCV

WAY DOWN DEEP, WE'RE ALL MOTIVATED
BY THE SAME URGES. CATS HAVE THE
COURAGE TO LIVE BY THEM.

JIM DAVIS

YOU CAN'T OWN A CAT.
THE BEST YOU CAN DO IS BE PARTNERS.

SIR HARRY SWANSON

ALL CATS ARE POSSESSED OF A
PROUD SPIRIT, AND THE SUREST WAY
TO FORFEIT THE ESTEEM OF A CAT IS
TO TREAT HIM AS AN INFERIOR BEING.

MICHAEL JOSEPH

The Monster Game

How do games with pets get started anyway? Is it their idea or ours?

One day I walked into the family room and Miss Middy sat there, wide-eyed, alert, obviously in a playful mood. She froze into a position of readiness to run, much like a dog who wants you to throw his ball. She gave a little false start, but remained in her spot. Taking the cue, I stalked toward her, arms outstretched in a zombie pose. She ran across the room at breakneck speed with me lumbering in hot pursuit. She ducked behind the couch, meowing mournfully in mock fear, but loving every minute of it. I hit the couch soundly and boomed, "I'm going to get you!" She ran out the other end, streaked across the room, and hid behind a chair. She peeked at me with wide eyes, making sure I was still in the game. When I advanced, she scampered into the hallway, feet slipping wildly on the tile, as I chased her through the living room, the dining area, the kitchen, and back into the family room.

When she finally tired (I was already exhausted!), she dropped to her knees in front of me in surrender, with head bent low. I scruffed her fur by rubbing it roughly from head to tail, still threatening her in a low voice, "I've got you. I am a monster and I'm going to eat you up—such a tasty morsel! Yum! Yum!" She stiffened her neck and back, flattened her ears, and raised her head for me to rub it harder, all the time emitting loud wails.

That's how Miss Middy's favorite game was born—"The Monster Game," as Jerry and I called it. A powerful game formed by active imagination.

We soon discovered that the best part of the game for Middy was the brisk rubdown following surrender. Sometimes after we'd barely begun the game she'd drop almost immediately into position for the best part, the fur on her back rippling in anticipation. During the rubdown she still played out her role by yowling in mock terror.

This eventually became our nightly routine where it culminated in our king-size bed with Middy running and hiding under the sheets, snuggling up to Jerry for protection. He'd wrap his big arms around her and say, "Come here, honey, I won't let the monster get you." By the time I crawled into bed, the two of them would be sound asleep, Middy's front paws wrapped tightly around Jerry's arm where she felt safe and secure.

Lying there in bed, I succumbed to my own mental monster games—ugly fears slashing at my heart and chasing me down dark corridors of possibility where I cringed in terror. But it was no fun. And it certainly was no game.

Three years after his radiation treatments, Jerry's cancer returned with a vengeance. During the six months following his last routine CAT scan, a huge, inoperable mass had developed near his aorta for which he was undergoing extensive chemotherapy. In such fertile soil of reality, it is easy for monstrous fears to spring up. After tossing and turning, exhausted by running from my fearful "what ifs?" I'd finally turn to my Lord in surrender and seek His loving touch. Like Middy, I could then rest peacefully, safe and secure in my heavenly Father's arms of protection—soothed to sleep by His promises.

Lord, during the dark stretches of life's journey, please give me courage to face my monsters in the light of Your reality. Remind me that whatever happens, You are in control and nothing can separate us from Your love. Amen

Don't be afraid, because I have saved you.
I have called you by name, and you are mine.
When you pass through the waters, I will be with you.
When you cross rivers, you will not drown.
. . . I, the LORD, am your God,
the Holy One of Israel, your Savior.
. . . you are precious to me
. . . I give you honor and love you.

ISAIAH 43:1-4 NCV

THE PROBLEM WITH CATS IS
THAT THEY GET THE SAME EXACT
LOOK WHETHER THEY SEE A MOTH
OR AN AXE MURDERER.

PAULA POUNDSTONE

CATS DO NOT HAVE TO BE SHOWN
HOW TO HAVE A GOOD TIME, FOR THEY
ARE UNFAILING INGENIOUS IN THAT RESPECT.

JAMES MASON

HE HAS BECOME A MUCH BETTER CAT
THAN I HAVE A PERSON. WITH HIS GENTLE
URGINGS, HE MADE ME REALIZE THAT LIFE
DOESN'T END JUST BECAUSE ONE HAS
A FEW OBSTACLES TO OVERCOME.

MARY F. GRAF

Epilogue

Miss Middy watches with interest as the bright-colored koi join in a feeding frenzy in the backyard pond. She and I moved to this smaller place after Jerry went home to heaven more than two years ago. Jerry and I had forty-seven wonderful years together—and forty-seven years of loving our cats.

Miss Middy and I still play games, love each other, and snuggle in front of the TV where she intently watches cartoons when it's her turn to choose.

Sometimes I am asked, "Do you think our pets will go to heaven?" My opinion is yes. Do I say this simply because I want it to be, or is there biblical evidence to support such an idea?

In his book *Heaven*, Randy Alcorn writes:

> Isaiah anticipates an eternal Kingdom of God on earth. Isaiah 65:17 and 66:22 specifically speak of the New Earth. Sandwiched between them is a reference very similar to that in Isaiah 11: "The wolf and the lamb will feed together, and the lion will eat straw like the ox . . . They will neither harm nor destroy . . .' says the LORD" (65:25 NIV). These descriptions of animals peacefully inhabiting the earth may have application to a millennial kingdom on the old Earth, but their primary reference appears to be to God's eternal Kingdom, where mankind and animals will enjoy a redeemed earth.

Yes, I believe our beloved pets will be in heaven. I believe that each of our cats, Curiosity, Smokey, Single Strength, and El Gato Gordo will be waiting there—with all whom we love—when Miss Middy and I arrive. And why shouldn't they? As feline members of our earthly family, God chose to use them to help train another Kitty—the author of this book.

CATS

God knew there'd be times
When we'd need a friend—
A soft gentle creature
Who'd love to the end.
A friend who has grace,
and patience and class.
So He searched all of heaven
And then sent us cats.

KITTY CHAPPELL